Crip Stories

BS Windon is a neurodivergent writer of Wiradjuri descent based in Naarm. He writes quirky stories about quirky people and all of the dark goo living inside him. He is more confident on a stage in front of an audience than in social gatherings.

Laura Pettenuzzo (she/her) is a disabled writer, speaker and accessible communications professional living on Wurundjeri land. Her work explores disability pride, systemic and internalised ableism as well as the power of self-acceptance. Her reviews, memoir and opinion pieces have been published in places such as *Griffith Review*, *Archer Magazine*, *Meanjin* and *The Age*.

Misbah Wolf (she/they) is a CALD neurodivergent multi-dimensional artist living in Naarm. She writes books and poetry, performs, teaches, researches, and creates. Her creative work, which explores love, be/longing, ghosts, and wildness – anything gothic – has appeared in many places.

Katie Hansord (she/they) is a neurodivergent and queer writer and researcher in Naarm. Her interests include poetry, gender, disability, and print cultures, and her writing has been published in *Mascara*, *Unusual Work*, *LOR Journal*, and the Long Paddock, *Southerly Journal*.

'Weaving together audacious truth-telling, tender lyricism, startling humour and uncategorisable wildness, *Crip Stories* leaves all the stale tropes about disability and neurodivergence far behind in the dust. These stories create a myriad of alluring desire lines for us all to follow, and artful, handcrafted bowers in which to find rest along the way. A spacious resource for now and for the future.'

Andy Jackson

'*Crip Stories* is the perfect kaleidoscope of human experience, shimmering and illuminating; it is an absolute gift to read.'

Fiona Murphy

'Refreshing takes from the criptastic community I know and love. *Crip Stories* welcomes the reader into a shared divergent consciousness. Radical, radiant and raring to rip the mould to shreds. Far more real than condescending disability trauma porn, this collection embraces and eviscerates, rebuilding perspective outside the pervasive ableist lens.'

Jasper Peach

Crip Stories

An Anthology of Disabled Writers

A *Mascara Literary Review* Anthology

Edited By
BS Windon, Laura Pettenuzzo,
Misbah Wolf, Katie Hansord

UNSW Press acknowledges the Bidjigal people, the Traditional Owners of the unceded territory on which the Randwick and Kensington campuses of UNSW are situated, and recognises the continuing connection to Country and culture. We pay our respects to Elders past and present.

A NewSouth book

Published by
NewSouth Publishing
University of New South Wales Press Ltd
University of New South Wales
Sydney NSW 2052
AUSTRALIA
https://unsw.press/

First published 2026

A catalogue record for this book is available from the National Library of Australia

ISBN: 9781761170478 (paperback)
9781761179365 (ebook)
9781761178627 (ePDF)

Cover design Regine Abos
Cover image Meagan Pelham, *Pinky Pinky Parrot*, 2024, **studio A**
Internal design Josephine Pajor-Markus

This project has been assisted by the Australian Government through Creative Australia, its principal arts investment and advisory body.

Published in association with *Mascara Literary Review*.

Contents

Acknowledgement of Country

We acknowledge the Traditional Custodians of the land on which this anthology was developed; the Wurundjeri people of the Kulin Nation, the Palawa people of Lutruwita, and the people of the Dharug Nation. We pay our respects to their Elders, past and present, and give thanks for their continued care of Country. As there are writers in this anthology from all across the land, we'd like to extend that acknowledgement to all Traditional Owners and First Peoples of so-called Australia. This is, was, and always will be: Aboriginal Land.

We honour their enduring connection to Country, storytelling, culture, and creative expression – which continue to guide and shape this land, and we pay our deepest gratitude to the ongoing storytellers, activists, Elders, and all of the resilient, emerging First Nations storytellers of the future.

We encourage readers to consider where they're reading this anthology from. Take a moment to hold heart and warmth for the Traditional Owners of the land they're currently on and reflect on the effects of colonisation on Country and culture. This land would be a very different place with the proper respect shown to the First Peoples who have inhabited this land for thousands of years.

We express our humblest thanks for the effort and devotion that they have put into caring for Country, cultivating culture, and yarning an undeniable presence that is unique among the world.

With this, we pay our deepest respects to Elders, past and present, and extend that respect to all Aboriginal and Torres Strait Islander peoples.

Sovereignty was never ceded.

This is, was, and always will be Aboriginal land.

A statement of solidarity with Palestine

As an essential time-bound declaration we editors should also like to express our deep solidarity with the ongoing struggles of Palestine sovereignty, and our hearts go out to all families and individuals who have experienced and are still undergoing not just continued invasion/colonisations since 1948 but continue to fight, live, and demand, even in their darkest hours, a right to their homeland, to their ancestral trees, houses, stories, culture, and freedom.

Dandelion seeds and glitches in the matrix: Thoughts from the editors

We open with an invitation: let these stories be eruptions. Let them be refusal. Let them move crookedly, glitch, spiral, laugh, rage, and shimmer. Let them be unapologetically crip – nonlinear, sensory, noncompliant. In a world increasingly flooded by algorithmic sameness, we need this reminder: meaning is not seamlessness. Meaning is contradiction, process, refusal, love, politics, justice, poetry, rupture.

This book is absolutely a celebration. Crip stories are not only about resistance, but also about joy, creativity, tenderness, community, and pride. To tell our stories is to declare: we are not symptoms. We are not metaphors. We are here, making futures.

We offer *Crip Stories* as a counterweight to erasure and as an invitation to possibility. To enter is to witness not only disabled stories, but disabled ways of telling stories – embodied, resistant, playful. Disabled storytelling disrupts and unsettles. It refuses to be flattened into productivity metrics or 'inspiration porn'. It challenges the very foundations of what literature and art are expected to do. Disabled writing is not a supplement to the literary establishment – it sets the whole damn thing off-kilter. It is innovation personified.

As a team, we recognised that the work of confronting internalised ableism takes many forms. For Misbah, a late-diagnosed AuDHD person, it meant un-gaslighting herself from the quiet, constant sense of not being 'quite right'. She writes of decolonising the self-loathing she carried, and of catching the words once used to describe herself – mad, crazy, too much, not enough – words that had worked as microaggressions, turned inward and outward. Her reflection reminds us how deeply systemic ableism is woven into our language, and how powerful it is to reclaim it, not as pathology, but as survival and pride.

Wiradjuri editor BS Windon helped to curate some exciting work from First Nations writers in this project. Mob voices are often a token inclusion, so BS Windon was thankful that right from the beginning of this project they would have a prominent platform to share as much of themselves as they desire.

Why this book, why now?

This anthology joins a long lineage of disabled storytelling. We honour the writers, activists, and communities who cracked open the canon, fought for access, and told stories outside official archives. *Crip Stories* adds to the proliferating global field of disability literature, which has seen huge growth especially over the past ten years. This development reflects a much-needed flourishing of anthologies centring creative writing by disabled people. Simultaneously, and just as importantly, this has meant centring lived experience of disability, as told by people *actually* experiencing it. This has also meant increased literary visibility and advocacy for and by the disability community, challenging the rampant experiences of harm, stigma, dehumanisation, ableism, inaccessibility, shaming, exclusion, and misinformation. Anthologies such as the groundbreaking *Disability Visibility: First-person stories from the twenty-first century*, edited by Alice Wong in 2020 (Alice passed away in 2025, leaving an incredible legacy of disability justice, activism and presence), and Australian counterparts such as *Growing Up Disabled in Australia* (2021), edited by Carly Findlay, through to more recent anthologies including *We've Got This: Stories of disabled parenting* (2022), edited by Eliza Hull; *Raging Grace: Australian writers speak out on disability* (2024) edited by Andy Jackson, Esther Ottaway and Kerri Shying; and *Someone*

Like Me: An anthology of non-fiction by autistic writers (2025), edited by Clem Bastow and Jo Case, are all doing important work to make more space for disabled writers' voices, and for disability justice in the world. With each iteration of stories shared comes a greater understanding of the importance of lived experience representation.

Moving beyond ideas of representation alone, this current anthology brings in a structural allyship pushing back against barriers faced by First Nations and disabled authors of colour in particular. Questions around whose voices are typically privileged and centred, and whose are excluded, silenced, or appropriated, are central to this. The hundreds of amazing submissions we received for this anthology are testament to the huge need for this kind of space, for speaking back to injustices and sharing lived experiences through the power, truth and beauty of creative disabled writing by multiply marginalised writers. We have tried to represent as wide a variety of multiply marginalised disabled experiences as possible.

In Australia, First Nations storytelling is foundational – ancient and futuristic, carrying survival despite colonisation and reminding us this land was never ceded. The Wiradjuri voices here, alongside that of Dulgubarra-Yidinji writer Skye Cusack, ground the collection in truths that reverberate, surpass, and thrive beyond colonial invasion and attempted erasure while imagining new futures. We also stand with global disability poetics in recognising that disabled storytelling is always political, communal, and transformative.

You'll witness opposite ends of the experience spectrum in these pages with two Wiradjuri poets: the first professional publication for Sandra Collins, and work from the absolute living legend that is Kerri Shying. Both of these poets wowed us with their work and we're certain you'll find a lot in their poems as well.

Sharleigh Crittenden is an accomplished Wiradjuri writer whose first foray into the personal essay appears in this anthology. BS Windon had the honour of being there from the initial brainstorming, through multiple drafts that got more and more beautiful as they developed. Sharleigh's piece is a gorgeous display of vulnerability and we dare you to try not becoming emotionally engaged reading it.

Dulgubarra-Yidinji and Indonesian woman of many talents Skye Cusack shares work that had us cackling out loud every time we revisited it. Weaving thoughtful reflection with a sense of humour that deserves its own late-night talk show, Skye's storytelling acumen will assure you don't forget her name any time soon.

We also pause to honour Mario Licón Cabrera, who passed during the editing of this book. Mario's luminous sequence on encroaching blindness is one of the last works he completed. It does not ask for pity. Instead, it reframes sight into memory, fog, light, colour – absence as presence, loss as gift. His writing is numinous, generous, and deeply moving. It remains with us as record and offering, a place to leap from and dissolve into. We are grateful to include his words here, and we hold his memory in these pages.

Magic, pride and beauty

Magic happens when we come together. Understanding others in a deeper, more complex way allows us to understand ourselves better. And understanding ourselves is the key to contentment. That's what life is about. Contentment. Joy. Care. Even the most introverted person is better off when they know themselves and know others. It stirs something at our core; twists it into overnight oats of the most delicious variety. A rising tide lifts all ships and if you take our hands, we can conjure the magic needed to lift the tide.

Inside this book you will find an incredible variety of different stories, told in different ways, from perspectives you might not have any experience with. We encourage you to approach all of these pieces with an open heart – imagine, if you will, that you're wearing a pair of the author's shoes and walking alongside them in a field, holding hands, and humming a little tune. These authors have a desire to advocate and an excitement to reach out and touch readers (metaphorically).

We read far more incredible pieces than we were able to include in this anthology. We had to make some really difficult decisions and won't hesitate to say that if we had the funding and the power, this would be a ten-thousand-page epic featuring work from hundreds of disabled Australian authors.

Whether you love or hate these pieces, one thing is assured: they all evoke visceral reactions and promote the reality that no two disabled folk are the same. Despite common experiences (and there are a lot of those), we're all unique to ourselves and we should all be treated that way. And also kindness ... being treated with kindness would be nice ... please.

At the heart of this anthology is disability pride. This means different things to different people, and we are not claiming to give you a definitive answer here. Broadly, disability pride emerged in response to the ableism disabled people face every day. It is a refusal to conform to ableist norms and expectations – of time, of labour, of relationships, of anything. It doesn't necessarily mean being proud of our disability – though for some people it can mean that. It involves a refusal to hide our disability or minimise our access needs for the comfort of nondisabled people.

We can't possibly write about disability pride without referencing poet and disability activist Laura Hershey's beloved poem, 'You get proud by practicing'. In it, Hershey offers readers a timeless invitation to view themselves anew, with grace and compassion. We've tried to embed disability pride into every element of this anthology. The title is one example. As disabled people, versed in the shifting language and politics of disability spaces, we were passionate about having the word 'crip' appear in some way in the title. Once a slur, it's an example of disabled people taking back something nondisabled people have used to 'other' and denigrate us: a linguistic testament to our refusal to conform, and to the beauty in our otherness. On that note, some pieces contain distressing and disturbing language and content; this is part of our experience of the world, and we invite you to engage with it in a spirit of empathy.

In the early stages of this project, when we were getting to know each other, we started to call ourselves the 'Criptologists'. The name had a double meaning. We were dedicated to the examination of disabled stories, without a doubt, but we were also excavating these particular stories from the ableist crypt within which they'd lain for too long.

This introduction does not offer a single voice, but a chorus. It honours First Nations truth-telling, erupts in crip poetics, insists on pride, and situates this work within a lineage of disability literature. We hope you feel that chorus as you enter these pages – discordant at times, joyful at others, always unapologetically alive.

Criptacular Crippenings

Irina Frolova

Spoon Theory

I write to
the Dean of Students:
my psychology degree (three
years undergrad   plus Honours)
is in its tenth year   and I'm worried
I may need more time I say I have an access
plan and caring responsibilities and well life
with disability   in our family   spoons tend
to disappear amidst chaos and soul-searching
I ask where   they could have gone
swallow a spoonful of irony:
we are   the spoon theory
made tangible
yet   shame
sneaks   up
whispers   in
tongues – some
I grew up with
others I picked
up   on the way
like   tick bites
time goes by
in   peace talks
making   up
my mind a part
-time study of
what it means
to   be   human

Spirit

I dream of Takhi   their spikey manes rising
from the ochre of the Mongolian steppe

they move   unprized and untethered
along unseen trails

I like to imagine my distant ancestors
never touched them

here once a year the government asks R U OK?
are we?

once a year we walk Out of the Shadows
to prevent suicide and save lives

every other day I race the shadow
to the shade of gum trees

trace time from the roots to the branches
note the freshly stripped bark

the calligraphy on scribbly gums
holding stories of perseverance

never in neat lines
the defiant dance

of decay   fallen and darkened
trunks in tight embrace with mycelium

by the lily-pond I ponder writing haiku
but each moment is water

trees peer into the rippled glass
shrugging their shoulders   while

the white cockatoos screech into the blue
ever-changing   everlasting

hear
hear!

I listen to their everyday
resistance

follow
a trail of my own

Notes

Spoon Theory refers to a concept by Christine Miserandino that uses spoons as a metaphor for the amount of energy someone has on any given day.

Takhi, meaning 'spirit' in Mongolian, also known as Przewalski's horse, is believed to be the last true wild horse in the world.

Out of the Shadows Walk is an annual Australian fundraiser for World Suicide Prevention Day.

Sharleigh Crittenden

Going in circles

It starts as an attack of vertigo – a scarcely perceptible swaying on my feet – then expands to a contraction in my field of vision: fuzzy spots float in my right eye, blanking out shoulders, arms, even the faces of my children from certain angles.

I know the signs, my body having long ago offered up their meaning: I have about fifteen minutes to get my hands on some soluble aspirin. My stomach muscles are already weakening, and my body's ability to absorb medication is rapidly declining. Once the headache sets in, I will be in gastric stasis and then there's no budging it, only bunkering down and waiting for it to pass. I turn anxiously towards my mother-in-law – who is five-maybe-six feet behind me and off to the left – trying to judge how easily I can get around this swell of people to reach her. They move like a current around me. I see a gap open up and dart through it.

Her brow furrows. She has no aspirin. Stupidly, I haven't brought mine with me. I sweep the crowd for my aunty-in-law. She drives the car – if we can't find someone nearby who has aspirin, she could drive to the nearest pharmacy. It's possible she could make it in time. I watch helplessly as she asks a few nearby women. A few of them shake their head – holding their hands upwards in gestures that suggest emptiness. One woman nods vigorously before producing a blister pack of ibuprofen capsules. When I see the label, I shake my head. Once more she excavates her handbag, this time offering up a sleeve of paracetamol tablets. Capsules and tablets take much longer to enter the bloodstream through the stomach. They don't stand a chance.

'Thank you,' I say, 'but no.'

I feel time slipping away from me but I can't say how long before it's too late and the entire day is lost. My aunty-in-law climbs into the car and, as she pulls away, I feel the familiar pulsing pain taking up residence behind my left eye.

~~

I am lying in the artificial dark of the bedroom. Shades drawn. My in-laws keep my children occupied in the living room while I wait for the aspirin to work. I've misplaced my eye mask, so I have improvised and tied a navy scarf loosely around my head, covering my eyes. I hear my husband's voice. He's home early from his lunch meeting; he must have cut it short. I want to feel his arms around me. I haul myself up. As I shuffle into the room my daughter gets up from her seat at the coffee table, strewn with printer paper and coloured pencils, and holds out to me a sheet of paper, folded into a card.

'Here Mummy,' she says. 'I made this to help take your mind off of it.'

I take the card from her. Staring back at me, on the front of her card, is an enormous, unblinking eyeball. Inside the card, in her budding print, she has written *Dear mummy I Love you so so much.*

I thank her and stifle a laugh in case she misinterprets it as teasing (she is sensitive, like her mother). The very idea that she has drawn an eye to help distract me from the searing pain behind my own eye starts something fizzing in me.

I feel lighter.

Is it joy?

*

Together we sit in the living room and speculate on the migraine trigger – sleep deprivation, stress, hormones, the dramatic atmospheric changes of the last twenty-four hours. I feel pins and needles in the fingertips of my right hand. As we talk, it spreads quickly down my fingers to my hand and then my wrist. Now I can't feel my fingers at all. They feel stiff and foreign when I try to flex them.

'Honey?' I look from my hand to husband. 'I think I may be having a stroke.'

~~

I can't operate my phone well enough to summon Dr Google, so I toss it to my husband, who left his behind in the car. As his thumbs fly into action, I keep opening and closing my right hand, trying to stimulate blood flow in the way you do when you've been lying on a body part and it goes to sleep. The first words that tumble out of his mouth are 'hemiplegic migraine'. So, not a stroke (I breathe a sigh of relief).

As he reads out the symptoms of hemiplegic migraines, I mentally check off what I have been experiencing. The hemiplegia – weakness or paralysis to one side of the body, often the hand – typically occurs as part of the migraine aura, alongside other temporary neurological symptoms. It's one I haven't experienced before.

*

I don't remember my very first seizure. I *do* remember my first migraine. I woke in a darkened and unfamiliar room, in a quiet and unfamiliar house, with a pulsing and unfamiliar pain behind my eyes. I stumbled down the unfamiliar hallway into an unfamiliar bathroom. Alone, I hugged the toilet bowl and as I hurled into it I felt my loneliness amplified in the space between the cold tiles and white-hot nail of pain hammering into my head.

The following morning while I went about making my sandwich for school, I told my foster mother about it. She asked why I didn't wake her. My only thought was: *because I barely know you.*

Three weeks later she cornered me in my new bedroom and, using her body to block my access to the door, said she'd heard a rumour I'd been self-harming. What she'd really been doing (I later found out) was using the one friend I'd made – another fifteen-year-old girl who lived a couple of houses down on the same street – as a mole by recruiting the girl's mother. She now demanded to see it. I lifted my school shirt and folded down the top corner of my school skirt to reveal the lines I'd carved into my right hip. The look on her face when she saw the red lines that I'd arranged mindlessly into a star is burned into my mind. I can still hear the derision in her voice as she asked, rhetorically, 'What does *that* stand for? "Shar the star"?'

Within a week, I boarded a plane with my bags. A caseworker I'd never met collected me at the arrivals gate. We drove in silence. I consoled myself with the thought of reuniting with my sister. When my caseworker pulled in at a youth refuge in a different town, I didn't understand why she'd waited until she'd stopped the car to explain the situation to me. 'We haven't been able to find a placement at such short notice.'

My antidepressants, kept in a secure safe, are doled out in the mornings before breakfast and I swallow them while the refuge worker scribbles the time and dose into a ledger. At night, I lie awake with my door locked listening to the other inmates. Some nights their voices grow loud and wild, their private pain bubbling to the surface then boiling over. On a bad night, if one of them flips out, the night-shift worker calls the cops and we head to school tired and tense the next day. Ending up *here* – in this institution, masquerading as a home, with staff around the clock who collect pay cheques and feign care – was evidence that I was officially broken. Just like how, deep down, I've always felt that my body has been the problem: it has attracted unwanted attention, been disobedient and defective.

*

I arrange a telehealth consult with my current GP. Specialists like neurologists require referrals every twelve months. Medications like anti-epileptic drugs (AEDs) require a specially authorised prescription. Without seizure control, my risk of SUDEP (sudden unexpected death in epilepsy) increases. Being Aboriginal also increases my risk for epilepsy-related death threefold. My GP emails me a referral and when I open it, I see he has also requested some blood work. More specifically, he has requested blood serum levels for my anti-epileptic medication.

My heart sinks.

*

Obtaining blood serum levels for AEDs is a method of testing the concentration levels of medication in the bloodstream. As far as I can make out, it is a practice built on the premise that there is a set therapeutic (or ideal) blood concentration range that can be measured by blood tests. This means that the level of anti-epileptic drug in the bloodstream is enough to prevent seizures but not enough to be toxic. The stated purpose of this blood test, then, is to ensure the correct dose. Another apparently legitimate purpose described in the literature on AED blood monitoring, though it has never been mentioned by my healthcare team, is ensuring compliance.

But to me, it feels unacceptably invasive.

It feels as though I am being policed, and it breaks the compact of trust between neurologist and patient.

~~

Many Aboriginal people wish to avoid surveillance as much as possible. It has to do with the ways our bodies are policed and controlled.

On my way home from work last night, at the Chalmers Street entrance to Central Station, an Aboriginal man was being searched by police. He stood submissively, legs apart, hands on the back of his head. The officers had guns and he did not. To afford him the dignity he deserves, I averted my gaze as the first officer patted him down while the second stood watch. I considered, for just a second, walking over and asking the man if he was okay, but I'm keenly aware that interrupting police is not a safe thing for me to do.

I've listened as family members recounted late-night bail checks from police that put their private rental arrangements at risk when their housemate was forced to haul themselves out of bed on a work night to answer the door. I think about the ways my own body has been controlled and moved around, like the year my sister and I hit puberty, and our first 'carer' shuffled us off to the GP to get prescriptions for contraceptive pills – presumably striking pre-emptively at the mere possibility of teenage pregnancies.

A familiar fury at my own powerlessness growls in the pit of my stomach.

~~

I have become adept at contorting myself to fit in, adept at functioning on a few hours of sleep, at navigating through hemiplegic migraines to get through social obligations, adept at apologising to others: 'sorry that I don't seem able to hold a conversation', 'sorry if I seem a bit off, I had a seizure', 'sorry I can't meet you for lunch today, I'm not feeling well'.

When people learn about my childhood, about the stint of homelessness and living in a youth refuge and moving between different foster homes and spreading the HSC over two years just to get through it and the second stint of homelessness in my first year of law school, they act surprised. They say, 'You seem so normal.'

What they don't see is the weekends I'm bound to my bed because, yet again, I've overextended myself. They don't see the twelve seizures I had in 2023 as I finished my law degree and simultaneously cared for two children under four, while writing reports and presenting at conferences.

Over the years, many friends and colleagues have suggested I have ADHD, especially recently, as adult diagnoses of ADHD become more common as public awareness of the neurodivergence paradigm increases. Several years ago, before my epilepsy diagnosis, I raised ADHD with my GP at the time, who merely waved his hand dismissively. While I wouldn't go so far as to say that I'm self-diagnosed, I *would* say that many of the struggles and strengths associated with ADHD resonate with me. But for girls, the signs are often overlooked. Old school reports noted a tendency to go off task, to become distracted, to talk too much. But they also noted my enthusiasm for learning, and my openness to being 'redirected'. Year after year, educators described my struggle as one of discipline and organisation. *If Sharleigh could only attend to her homework tasks – if she could manage her time better during exams – she might reach her full potential.*

On the face of it, I did meet my potential. I finished school and even graduated from my arts degree with distinction. But what isn't visible is the two years I spent doing the HSC instead of one, or the twelve-and-a-half years it took to finish my double degree. Sometimes I can't help but wonder if this would have played out differently had my GP at the time taken me seriously. After decades of trying, it is clear to me now that effort alone is not enough for me to wrangle chaos into order.

So, why not pursue a formal diagnosis?

My experience as an Aboriginal woman and survivor of the out-of-home care system also influences my choice as to whether and to what extent I decide to subject myself to the medical model, including whether or not to pursue an ADHD diagnosis.

Also, I feel I have enough formal diagnoses to last me a lifetime – not only epilepsy but complex post-traumatic stress disorder (C-PTSD) and endometriosis and now, hemiplegic migraines. Instead, I wrap myself in my husband's observation that my excitable nature is how I'm able to lock in on people, to establish a swift rapport so they feel interesting, and important. He offers me acceptance in the playful nod at the pile of clothes multiplying on my side of the bed. These things speak of my joy and my chaos as intertwined and inseparable, yet he foregrounds the joy and, in doing so, allows me to see myself differently. It speaks to my wholeness.

*

I'm not normal. I'm good at putting on the face of normal, at presenting what I expect others want to see, because when I have presented my authentic self in the past, I have been moved on, derided and torn down.

I keep thinking that, if I just keep writing, some kind of sense will emerge from it all.

But maybe that's the real lesson here. We go on in ever-widening or ever-narrowing concentric circles without ever really connecting with a universal truth.

The truth is I have a long way to go. There is an enormous period of reckoning ahead as I attempt to come to terms with the conditions of my life, with its possibly permanent limitations. When I received my epilepsy diagnosis in late 2017, I had to give up driving. It continues to make the logistics of raising children challenging. I often rely on my in-laws to help me get to where we need to go. But they are getting older. One day, they will give up driving altogether. When we travel as a family for holidays or short trips, my husband will be behind the wheel the whole time and, though I know he is happy to, I catch myself thinking about the time we road tripped to Armidale in 2016, and how it felt to have control over the car, to steer it where I wanted it to go, to take it in turns. Sometimes I worry about not pulling my weight. I even make choices about my medical team based on geographic accessibility. I now see a GP within walking distance of my home. I've begun to accept that I may never be well enough to work a full-time job. I worry about disclosing my condition to employers and colleagues. I worry that it will shape the way they perceive me.

I try to balance these fears and losses with what I do have: a circle of close friends who are forgiving of my forgetfulness, or periods of lapsed communication, or cancelled catch-ups. I have new colleagues who encourage me to set healthy boundaries in my work life. I've been honestly considering my capacity before making new commitments. As a result, I've been practising saying 'no' more in the last few months.

~~

Recently, I've found myself wondering who I would be without the distortions caused by the things that have been done to me as a child and as a young person. With my family – my husband, and my children – I see that person beginning, now, in my thirties, to emerge – a person who is deeply sensitive. Meeting myself where I am, like acceptance, is hard. Bit by bit, I am beginning to feel like my own person.

I see that person reflected back at me in my daughter, who just today cried her little heart out as her teacher led her, along with her classmates, in two tidy lines away to the classroom. As she looked over at me from across the playground, I felt the impulse to dash over to her and fold her into my arms, but I'd just been chastised by her teacher, who took her hand from mine and nestled her back into her spot in the neat line. As I summoned a brave, reassuring smile for her, I tried to remind myself that she hasn't had my life experiences – her mother is alive. I try to remind myself that what she will need when she's home today is not to be shunted off to do her homework, but to be folded lovingly in my arms after six hours of holding it together.

My children are accustomed to their mother being unwell for periods. They are used to Mummy needing to take a rest. Words like *migraine* and *seizure* are part of their vernacular. I often find myself hoping that my children will grow up to be compassionate people – to themselves and others – as a result. That they will learn, by observation, or osmosis, the value in rest and in not habitually pushing themselves, and others, beyond their physical and psychological capacity.

I hope they also look on what I've managed to achieve, slowly and with small but accumulating steps, and know that there is choice, that they can they choose how to channel their energies, but that their lives are valuable irrespective of their 'output'. Admittedly, a lesson I'm still learning myself.

~~

In the shower now, I look down at that spot on the inside of my right hip and I see the year I turned eighteen and returned, for the first and the last time, to my hometown for a funeral. I see the year I got my brother to tattoo over the old scars that, by then, had silvered with age. In another language, I'd scribbled out the words *keep faith* for him to etch onto my skin – a code that allowed me to keep the words safe from probing eyes – and, though the blade marks were still faintly visible beneath the ink (because scar tissue doesn't tattoo well), it was a contract I made with myself. Now, after growing and birthing two children, my body is adorned with a series of stretch marks and a fresh layer of story has been laid down over the old messages, obscuring and overwriting them. When I look at this part of my body, I no longer feel the shame or grief as acutely.

The shame was given to me, but it was never mine to carry.

Sandra Collins

Sweet surrender

Feeling disheartened

Empty . .   .   .   .   . cold

Isolated

A gaping absence of connection to Country
Ancestors bring compressed, silent wailing from deep inside me.

Holding on ... holding on for decades
Now exhausted I can no longer maintain my vigilant control.

My wailing is a songline
vibrating across country with earthquake intensity.

Gravel slides, stones fly, rocks shake, earth splits.

Absolute silence ... can you hear it?

An east breeze arrives ... blowing dust, leaves rustle, branches sway ...
Kingfisher sings.

And there she is ... by the campfire
Her eyes seek me first
hold me fast
I barely breathe in her presence
In ancient ways she offers me my birth right.

I give over
She channels it all into me

Expanding, my heart pumps wildly
I am alive!
Opening to earth, sky, fire, water, air – all nature
S l i d i n g into the shoes of my Elder MamaGirl

We are one
        Connected now
Whole

Collapsing into her arms with love
She's always waiting for me

Angela Costi

Reporting back to MRI

Slipped in like a pill on a tongue. But not swallowed. Stilled. As if frozen in flight. Made to play dead while I hear belches, gurks, farts, burps without apology. As if there's a troupe of hungover archaeologists traipsing through my internal topography, falling into my canals, emerging wet with my grief's debris.

The myometrium appears heterogeneous

No free fluid identified in the pouch of Douglas

A 53x43x44 mm hypoechoic solid lesion
at the left ovary
with internal vascularity

Each report arrives with a rare find.

The one delivered on 08/04/2023 is printed and ready for me to read. I have not read it at the date of this poem, 24/08/2024.

Between my body and the six neglected pages to the right of my monitor, is a metaphor for fear. The time I was four running into the night's long corridor looking for the toilet, unable to see, searching for a door with something getting bigger and bigger, smashing through the dark, coming for me.

MULTIPLE SCHWANNOMA
5.5x4.5 cm
R side of spine

Baba said, if you prod in tunnels and wells, you will find things that shouldn't be there.

It is not understood why multiple schwannomatosis occurs. People have looked into a number of genetic mechanisms, but it is not fully understood.

The lesion in the paraspinal region is a Schwannoma.

Early degenerative changes in the thoracic spine.

As at 25/09/2025, my breathing is regular, there is a slight ping in my left thigh as the lime-sized one jostles for space, I touch it through my cotton pyjamas, it soothes itself back to sleep

Earthing

The neurosurgeon is my ally   together we battle
with me playing dead   in a theatre
of scalpels and scissors

grind my teeth whenever
he and *genetic counsellor*
call my growths   *schwannomas*

surgical fists   close in on the big one
daring to oust my spine

my body is their strange planet
making bombs from nerve sheaths to strike
when least expected

After the dulling of pain   masked faces
speak in coded whispers
use therapies to waken my legs

sessions to quieten my breath
a new counsellor enters without clipboard
touches the ache of my childhood

I exhale the diagnosis
make it   orbit   far
far away

use my journal to travel from hospital
to house   look at the view each window offers

of Earth   raw with its burnt and fallen

Excavate or occupy

weeds infiltrate organs
          worms grow the length of intestines
parasite hierarchies   cross borders of skin

the lesions are said to infiltrate
          stabilised for now
numbered   uniformed   badged

within the MRI   I am the island
of silent flutters
          as mind walks me to lakes and mountains

my cells mutate happily
                                        among the ebbs and flows
of burrowing

as naked mole-rats do
without sight   hair   muscle
              they continue to live with cancer as their quiet friend

they are probed   by science to measure *how freaky*
still they live for over thirty years
                                    if left to keep their spleen and marrow

defective genes march on
cannot be shrivelled by laser
my surgeon continues to make discoveries

from medulla to coccyx
he excavates these rare deposits
gifted by ancestry

Hannah Hall

The changing room

There is a particular kind of heat that radiates from the concrete of a public swimming pool. It incites quick steps – no running! – feet finding the cool of the poolside tiles and then the water. A rite of passage over hot coals. Contrast therapy for the uninitiated suburban masses. Heated dashes make this spectacle of summertime ecology almost comical. Old bodies, teenage struts, wrinkles, drooping, bulges, swollen bellies and new-found breasts, all jogging, tiptoeing towards the cool water. In no other context in society do we see this kind of variety and display of the human body. A moveable exhibition of biology.

I'm eleven years old and the new girl in town. Those two things aside are enough to make an afternoon at the pool an excruciating experience. Bathers never seem to sit right, either too dowdy or too tight and showing a body you don't yet understand. The untrained eyes of teenaged boys might stare, or not stare – you're not sure which is worse.

I'm meeting some friends at the pool, a typical thing for pre-teen girls to do in summer, and something I feel like I can't keep saying no to. These new friends know me well enough from school, but they don't really know me. They don't know me like this – open, on display, nothing to hide behind, no more made-up excuses.

I see my friends run in, waving back towards an idling station wagon across the road. They head past the metal turnstiles and towards the changing rooms. I hang back, standing at the edge of the pool, nudging the rounded edge with my shoe; the water waves lightly in the wind making a pattern that almost sucks me into its depths.

My friends yell to hurry up, come on. I step down and follow them to the changing rooms. In an instant, my bathers don't feel so tight anymore, my thighs don't seem so doughy. All I can think about is when they see me, they'll see I'm different – defective. Their looks will tell me I am abnormal. Malformed. An abomination. Wrong.

I was born with a deformity, a physical difference. The bones in my toes, pinky fingers and elbows bend at angles that deem me disfigured. My deformity is most severe in my feet. At birth my toes splayed out at right angles towards the opposite foot, webbed skin stretched taut between my big toes and second toes. My bones malformed in utero to the point that they didn't work functionally as feet or pass as aesthetically acceptable human features.

When I was a baby, my mum would cover and wrap me up so my feet were hidden from visitors. When my granddad came to meet me for the first time a few days after my birth, he instinctively started to unwrap the blankets I was in to see 'what was going on', like he would check under the hood of the old Commodore. My mum snatched me away from him, furious, and wrapped me up again. She told me about this when I was in my late twenties, on the eve of my most recent orthopaedic surgery. She said she knew he was probably just curious, just wanted to know everything about his new granddaughter. Her instinct, however, was to protect me from any kind of judgement, and in order to do that she covered me up – hid my deformity.

It was a few weeks after my first birthday when I had my first surgery to 'correct' the medically declared 'wrong' of my deformity. I'd just started trying to walk, which must have seemed both ironic and cruel to my parents as they wheeled me towards the paediatric surgery wing of the hospital. My tiny, crooked feet and I were about to undergo an intense surgery where all my toes would be broken so they could then be reset in a less deformed, less disfigured, more socially acceptable configuration, but also one that would help my growing bones to work in the way I needed them to.

After the six-hour surgery, I was still deformed, but recast slightly, my broken bones forming a new difference that I would wear for the next two decades of my life. I spent twelve weeks with casts on from my knees to an inch beyond my feet to cover the metal pins that had been hammered into my toes to keep them in place while they healed. My dad still has these pins – thick metal skewers about two inches long, sealed in a plastic specimen jar with a bright yellow lid. I remember this jar from when I was little; my dad kept them in his box of treasures and trinkets. He said they reminded him of how strong and brave I was, even as a baby. But I never felt that way – I just felt wrong and different and ashamed. I was even too ashamed to tell my dad how I felt, so instead I would just peer through the specimen jar like it was a looking glass, searching for something else in the distance, something far away. I wondered if they could use them again and make my feet 'normal' this time. Years later, when I would get my next surgery to realign my feet, they used metal pins again, but this time they were six inches long and thicker. There wasn't a big enough specimen jar to keep those ones in.

My deformity is a congenital condition called Clinodactyly. Its name comes from the Greek words 'klinein', which means to bend, and 'dactylos', which is the word for fingers or toes – digits of the body. A friendly orthopaedic surgeon once explained that to my mum and me in a consultation when I was eight or nine, and the phrase 'bent digits' has stuck with me ever since. I'd explain my condition to people using this translation or say the full medical term – Clinodactyly – pronouncing it like the name of a dinosaur, offering either a pterodactyl-like screech or the motion of T-rex arms. Even as a kid, I felt like I had to explain myself, that I needed to distract from or apologise for my abnormality. Quick, make the difference fun for them! Make it okay to wonder about.

A deformity or physical difference isn't inherently disabling, though it can be. In reality, it is the way society deals with difference that creates disabling factors. After my first surgery, the bone structure in my feet was straight enough to walk and run and even play sports badly (though that likely had more to do with my lack of interest than my feet). Medically speaking, my deformity doesn't qualify as a disability, and growing up I never considered myself disabled, or even deformed. Instead, I tried endlessly to ignore the fact that I was in some way *different*.

Despite what doctors might say, disability has always been a social construct rather than a physical manifestation. It is the result of societal prejudice, assumptions, and a long, cruel history based on the fallacy that is 'human normalcy'. Doctors see things through the medical model of disability, where humans and their human experience are reduced to symptoms, disorders and abnormalities. The medical model sees disability as something that is caused by the medical condition or physical qualities of a person. It perceives impairment as something to be fixed or changed, even if there is nothing inherently bad about living that way. This way of thinking about disability does not account for life itself, and what it is to live in the world when you are deemed medically or biologically divergent.

My parents never used the term 'deformed' – they would tell me that my feet were 'special'; that I was special because I was different, forgetting perhaps that to be 'different' is weird when you're a kid, and a curse when you're a teenager. My mum used to tell me that I had 'duck feet' and that's why I was so good at swimming – I wasn't; she was just trying to offer me some kind of silver lining to the misfortune of having to explain why my body was a certain way for the rest of my life. I know my parents spun this 'special' narrative on my deformity out of love, and perhaps also out of a desperate want for me to be okay with myself, to be happy. But ultimately this deflection reinforced the understanding I'd gleaned that I shouldn't show my difference, shouldn't celebrate it because 'special' and 'different' were synonymous for 'wrong' in the society I grew up in.

The more my parents lovingly told me it was okay, that I shouldn't worry about it, that I was being silly, the more I felt bad or wrong or undesirable because the world I was living in – at school, at swimming lessons, at pool parties, at dance class – did not share my parents' view of this 'special' difference. To most people, having a physical difference meant something had gone terribly wrong. At family days out at the beach, other mothers would stare at my feet, subtly pulling their own kids away as they passed. At dance class, the other girls would point, stare and move away from me, leaving me stranded, standing alone in the middle of the room, shifting awkwardly in my leotard and trying to cover one foot with the other and hide myself. After one semester, I didn't go back.

I wasn't prepared for experiences like this that directly contradicted my parents' narrative; I didn't have the understanding I do now of disability and difference and that it might be possible to be proud of it. Instead, these experiences bred shame, which caused decades of hiding and denying myself a full life experience for fear of this same kind of rejection. Unwittingly, by not ever naming it or acknowledging the difficulty it might bring because of the world we live in, my parents were the primary cause of my being disabled.

In the changing room of the local swimming pool, I calculated my fate as I slipped my shoes off and put them to one side. I hadn't mentioned anything about my deformity to my friends, but my mum said that it would be fine, that they would understand, and so surely, they would. Even so, I couldn't help but hold my breath as I took off my socks. As I stood up from the bench, I heard a scream and looked up to see one friend with her hands over her mouth, the other with a look of disgust and shock on her face. They both backed away from me and into the corner of the changing room.

And then, the questions.

What's wrong with you?
Why are they like that?
What *is* that?
What happened?

The disabled narrative that has no answer, only questions.

As they pressed themselves further against the tiled wall, I shrunk, and tried to explain myself, explain my deformity, that I was born with it, that they tried to fix it, telling them – and myself – it wasn't my fault, but knowing that it wouldn't make any difference.

They couldn't leave the changing room fast enough.

For the next hour or so, we swam in the pool, pretending it was another normal summer day. But every time I went near one friend she would recoil and jump on the other's back or swim away frantically, making some excuse not to be near me and my deformed body. Familiar questions started to pound.

Why am I different?
Why am I like this?
Why me?
What can I do about it?
Will I ever be okay?
Why does it hurt so much?
Why am I disgusting?
Why am I horrific?
Repugnant
Putrid
Bad
Broken
Wrong

When other people swam nearby, I would instinctively move my feet in tiny, furious kicks so that they might only see a blur of bubbles and kicks instead of seeing anything amiss with me or my body. I'd learnt how to hide it, or at least to try to distract from it when I could. I learnt how to run between the pool and changing rooms, between sea and sand with little, flicking steps so it might not be as obvious that I was defective. I'd dig my toes into the sand at beaches until I reached the shallows, and then I'd run in until it was deep enough so no-one could tell that, below the surface, I was defective, damaged, deformed. Run fast so they couldn't see me.

I left the pool that day knowing I never wanted to be looked at that way again. I saw the fear in my friends' eyes – the disgust, the horror and the repulsion. When they recoiled at the sight of me, I felt it like a stabbing pain. It confirmed what I had always suspected deep down inside – that I was inherently wrong and shameful.

And so, I decided to hide myself. I wouldn't accept any alternative, any solutions that parents or friends might offer. I grew a hard casing around all the self-perceptions I now knew to be true, knew that I was right all along. I would hide it all inside. I would not show people the monster I was. No matter what anyone told me.

Over the years, I thought constantly about the story of my feet. I thought about the fact that the surgeons didn't 'fix' me and about how many surgeries it would take to do that. I thought about how no-one would ever love me, probably. I thought about ways of mangling myself so they'd have to rebuild me and give me a full foot transplant and about how in the future that would be possible. I thought about how unfair it was that my brothers didn't have deformed feet when they never even wanted to wear pretty sandals like I did. I thought about how cruel the world was.

The experience of being physically disabled or deformed is often reduced to an over-medicalised list of features and symptoms. As a person with physical difference, your identity is often dictated by other people's perceptions, largely medical professionals, or your parents. You can easily lose agency of your own story, subscribing instead to the misinformation and internalised ableism that you're fed from a young age from both pop culture and culture at large.

Until I was in my late twenties, I'd never considered myself disabled. I spent a long time pushing down the questions about myself that, despite years of therapy, still manage to surge to the surface of my subconscious.

If I wasn't like this would I be brave and outgoing?
If I wasn't like this would I be in love?
If I wasn't like this would I be confident and sexy?
If I wasn't like this would I not wear boots when it's 40 degrees?
If I wasn't like this would I be popular and easy to talk to?
If I wasn't like this would I be happier?
If I wasn't like this would I be pretty?
If I wasn't like this would I be normal?
If I wasn't like this would I be okay?

Disability is a personal construct as much as it is a social one. How you translate each experience or diagnosis or bodily function (or lack thereof), makes up the complex form of your own identity. With each corrective surgery I have undergone, I have felt less deformed but somehow more disabled. Along with brutal scars and broken bones came the emotional pain of what it was I was trying to correct, and the impossibility of recovery from a life lived as 'different'. Disability is part of my existence largely because I fought so hard to deny it. Understanding the shame behind hiding my deformity has ultimately uncovered my reality of being disabled. Although my bones are misshapen, it is society's gaze that has truly deformed me. I think about how differently I might feel if I hadn't spent so many years hiding from my disability, and instead really dug down into the whys and the hows and the ways this could be different.

Opening up the emotional scar tissue of my deformity has also unveiled other disabilities and curiosities I live with – neurodivergent, autistic, bipolar, mad, crazy, weird. I can now embrace and accept so much more of myself, and know it is not a deficit. Society has not been kind to the deformed and disabled. It still isn't. But maybe by not ignoring it, I could have lived life a little more easily instead of in a perpetual state of internalised ableism and longing for unrealistic societal standards.

It's summer again, and I am standing at the edge of a pool, my feet firmly planted on the ground. I feel the sun scorching down on me, finding the bits that stick out – the tip of my nose, the tops of my shoulders, the line of my scalp where my hair is parted. Underneath my bare feet, the concrete burns just as hot as the sun. I notice the warm breeze and how it laps the water's surface. I see the disfigured line at the bottom of the pool, stretching from end to end.

And then I notice that I'm not hiding. I'm not bending my toes under, crushed to the ground so they can't be seen, or covering one foot with the other (the 'good' one).

I'm standing here and I'm eight years old at after-school swimming lessons. I'm standing here and I'm ten years old at my friend's pool party. I'm standing here and I'm fifteen, in my first boyfriend's bedroom, shoes off and lying close. I'm at the beach with friends, and in a dance class, and getting a massage in Thailand.

I'm standing in the changing room, and you can see me –

All of me

Just as I am.

I'm standing here and this time, I want you to see me.

Carly Findlay

Bodily grief

My curves withered away as the cancer let itself in without me noticing.
Slowly, sneakily remodelling this body into a shape I no longer recognise.
Straight up and down.
Floppy, frail, unfeminine.
I feel more teenage boy than an early middle-aged woman in this body.

Yet my face shows a sense of wellness –
sparkling eyes and a bright smile.
The most beautiful bald head.

'You look good considering;
it's amazing that you manage to put such great outfits together, despite,'
they say.

My facade defies the chemicals that surge within my body.
I look so well.

I check my hospital records to remind myself that
yes, I do have cancer.

In these times, it's only body positivity or body neutrality.
Social media and cancel culture is so harsh now,
that I don't even think people allow you to talk about weight loss or thinness in terms of illness.

There's only room for a certain size and shape in the body positivity
movement.
The rest of us beg to belong.

So I can't overtly state how I feel so very thin,
or that my thinness reminds me
that I am sick.

I can't talk about how I am now buying clothes
two sizes smaller than before my diagnosis.
Or how people tell me that being skinny is a good problem to have,
rather than the opposite, they say.
Well-meaning but unhelpful and fatphobic.

But I worry.
Because the weight loss is the only symptom of my cancer that has
stuck.
And I have two heaving wardrobes of clothes to be worn.

A twenty-five-centimetre tumour was removed,
I wonder where did it fit?
The tumour and my uterus were removed from my vagina –
It was the only way I'll ever give birth,
which means I'll never give birth.

My choice and chance were taken away because of cancer.
Body autonomy gone.

I giggle and wince thinking about my newly renovated reproductive
area.
Am I Barbie now?

Julie Dickson

Content warning: Derogatory use of the word 'midget'.

The 'M' word

You, like every person with dwarfism, can clearly remember the first time you were called the dreaded 'm' word – midget. The memory haunts you, and it still causes you to shudder. You were eighteen years old and had newly arrived in Melbourne from a small country town for uni. You were living at uni on-campus accommodation and were on the way to your aunt and uncle's house for dinner and to stay the night. But first, you made a detour to Ringwood Library to return a book. The library is tacked on to Eastland Shopping Centre – the first floor boasts a café, reception area, and art gallery. And then upstairs is the library. You successfully returned your library book upstairs, made it down the escalator and were walking to the exit when you heard it. A teenage boy snickered to his friends, 'Is that a midget?' You shuddered. You were no longer invisible. You were seen. You could feel his friends turn and stare at your back. 'It is too!' said one of his friends. 'Hey, midget!' one shouted. Then came the chorus, 'Midget!' 'Midget!' 'Midget!'

Your body instinctually kicked into flight mode – you fled. Your heart was racing, and your hands were clammy. Would they follow you? Would they come after you? There was a whole group of them, and there was only one of you. You had to get out of there. You power-walked out of the building. When you made it outside, you still didn't feel safe. You had to get out of there. You power-walked across the road to the train station and hopped on the train to go to your aunt and uncle's place. When the door shut and the train sped off and you looked around the near-empty carriage, with no teenage boys in sight, your shoulders could relax a little bit, but you were still in flight mode. You couldn't fully relax until you were safely inside your aunt and uncle's house.

The incident replayed itself in your mind over and over on the train ride. You were in a public place. There were staff at reception. There were other people milling about. Why did no-one stop them? Why did no-one call them out on it? Why did no-one check if you were okay?

You debated whether you should tell your aunt about it when you arrived at her place. You were embarrassed. If you told her, it would make it real. And you didn't want it to be real. You wanted to pretend it had never happened. So you kept it inside. When she asked you how your day was, you told her it was good and described the good things that had happened.

To understand the sting of the word 'midget', you have to look at its etymology. The word derives from *midge*, which Cambridge Dictionary defines as 'a small fly that flies in groups and often bites'.

In the 1700s, there were several performers with dwarfism in the United States of America. Charles Stratton, known by his performer name 'Tom Thumb', was the most well known. Eric D Lehman, in his book *Becoming Tom Thumb: Charles Stratton, PT Barnum, and the dawn of American celebrity*, writes that PT Barnum purchased Scudder's American Museum in New York in the 1800s and knew that 'physical oddities could sell tickets' (2013, p. 15), with people who were giant and people with dwarfism selling the most tickets. Charles Stratton was four when his parents took the job offered by PT Barnum, and Lehman writes he was given the stage name 'Tom Thumb' (2013, p. 17). The pay wasn't great, but jobs for people with dwarfism were limited, and people exploited him due to his age and disability.

Lehman writes that Charles Stratton was part of the 'Hall of Living Curiosities' (2013, p. 23) exhibition at the museum. PT Barnum strongly emphasised Tom Thumb's dwarfism as a spectacle and contributed to the public's negative perspective and attitudes towards people with dwarfism. This contributed to dehumanising people with dwarfism as objects, and PT Barnum later described Tom Thumb as a 'midget' (www.factmonster.com). It's horrible to think that a person with dwarfism like myself was hired by a person of average height to be used as a spectacle, laughed at, and exploited with little pay.

Horrendous incidents like this have negatively shaped the public perception of people with dwarfism. The 2013 movie *The Wolf of Wall Street* directed by Martin Scorsese shows an example of 'dwarf tossing', where a group of stockbrokers gather in their office and people take turns throwing a person with dwarfism wearing velcro at a bullseye; a prize is offered for the one who sticks to the bullseye. The movie led many pubs to run similar 'midget tossing' events. Horrible events like this dehumanise people with dwarfism, treating them like objects instead of people, negatively shaping the public's perception of people with dwarfism and making it seem 'okay' to say no-one is watching you because they're too busy worrying about themselves and worrying about other people watching them. And you've always believed that to be true. Until the first time you were called the 'm' word in public. It struck you that that belief didn't apply to you. You were being watched. You were being seen. People noticed your dwarfism, and you were being negatively perceived as the 'other'.

You developed social anxiety. Everywhere you went, you were worried about people watching you. You could feel eyes on you. You noticed when kids looked at you, their eyes widening as they turned and did a double take, not quite believing their eyes, their stares lingering until their parents dragged them out of sight. When they would tug on their parents' hands and say, 'Mummy, Mummy, that girl is so little!' And their parents would shush them and drag them away.

Every time you saw a group of teenage boys, your heart would start racing, thinking they would notice you and shout out the 'm' word. So you would turn around and go back the way you came or find an alternative route.

You were called the dreaded 'm' word a second time. You were dressed up as a flapper on your way to your 1920s murder mystery–themed twenty-first birthday party. You had just gotten off the tram and walked past a group of men. One called out 'Midget!' and his friends joined in. 'Hey, midget!' 'Midget!' You shuddered and were immediately catapulted back to the first time you were called the 'm' word in public. Your heart was racing, and your hands were clammy. Again, you kicked into flight mode – you had to get out of there. You power-walked down the street, the blood rushing through your veins, not looking back. You kept walking until you made it to the bar and saw one of your friends. You went to the bathroom and pondered whether you should tell your friends what had happened. But again, you wanted to pretend it hadn't. And again, you thought, if you didn't tell anyone, you could pretend it wasn't real. So you took a few deep breaths, collected yourself, and went back into the function room to celebrate with your friends. But all throughout the party, the incident was at the back of your mind.

Being called 'midget' is triggering as it makes you think of all the times people with dwarfism were dehumanised in the past – such as Tom Thumb being put on display and made to perform at PT Barnum's museum and 'midget tossing' events where people with dwarfism are thrown at targets. It makes you feel like less of a person – like you're just an object for people to make fun of. You have to keep reminding yourself that you're worth more than that and you're not an object and to keep surrounding yourself with good people.

Before you were called the 'm' word the first time, you used to easily be able to go out in public without the fear of people watching you. Without the fear of kids staring and tugging their parents' arms to get their attention and without the fear of teenage boys shouting the 'm' word at you.

Every day you had to challenge these thoughts and push yourself to go outside, to go to a public place, to keep doing the things you needed to do like go to the supermarket, and the things you wanted to do, like go to a bookshop. The fear never quite subsided, and it still lingers, even to this day.

About six months or so after your first time being called the 'm' word, your friend messaged you asking if you wanted to hang out with her and go to a park in Ringwood. You happily agreed – it would be nice to spend time with her. After your trip to the park, she wanted to spend some time walking around the shops at Eastland and looking at the books in Ringwood Library. You froze – you hadn't been back to the library since the incident. You knew you'd have to go back there one day and ride over the bad memory with a good memory. To show yourself that it was a one-off, that it was a safe place / good place. This time, you weren't going to be alone. You'd be with your friend. Surely the same group of guys wouldn't be there, and if they were, they wouldn't make fun of you if you were with your friend. So you took a deep breath and went to the library. There wasn't a group of guys in the reception area. No-one shouted at you or called out to you or noticed you. Since then, you've been back to Ringwood Library a few times for write-ins with friends at the café and at the library.

You now realise that those times when you didn't tell anyone about being called the 'm' word because you didn't want to make it real – they had been real the whole time. Just because you don't tell someone about an incident doesn't mean it didn't happen; it doesn't mean it's not real. It *is* real. But by telling someone, the burden is shared and lifted, and it means you don't have to struggle with it on your own.

You've realised you shouldn't be embarrassed by these incidents. You shouldn't be embarrassed about having dwarfism and simply existing. The people who made fun of you for being a different body shape and for having a disability should be embarrassed by their behaviour.

There are times when you wish you had stood up for yourself. That you had turned around, walked up to the boys/men, told them how offensive the 'm' word is, and given them a lesson. But would they have listened? Would they have realised it was wrong, apologised, and agreed to never do it again? The second the 'm' word came out of their mouth, you knew they knew it was offensive by their tone. You knew they knew it was wrong. That's why they were doing it. They were doing it to get a reaction. And you weren't going to give them one.

You've since realised that walking away is an act of resistance. You've since realised it might not have been safe for you to stand up to them. There was only one of you and a group of them. They were taller and stronger than you and they could have fought back if you had stood up for yourself.

There needs to be more education on the 'm' word and how harmful it is and why it shouldn't be used. And in those moments, that was not the place to do it. It wasn't safe for you – the flight response kicked in for a reason: you had to get out of there.

Growing up, you were an avid reader and still are. You yearned to read books featuring characters who have dwarfism like you – to see yourself represented positively in fiction. There are few representations of people with dwarfism in books, movies, TV shows, and so on. And of those representations, very few are positive. People with dwarfism are often the butts of jokes, positioned as the 'other', infantilised or presented as inspiration porn.

These negative portrayals in the media are harmful because they normalise this behaviour and that this is the way to treat people with dwarfism, and this flows into how people treat people with dwarfism in everyday life.

Since there is very little positive representation of people with dwarfism in fiction, as a writer, you want to change that and write novels featuring protagonists who have dwarfism. You want to use your lived experience and that of your friends who have dwarfism to showcase positive and realistic representations of people with dwarfism.

You're currently writing a young adult novel about a teenage girl with dwarfism who goes on a road trip with her friends to meet other people with dwarfism who will help her decide if she should take a drug that could make her taller. In it, you explore the negative implications of being called 'midget' and the lasting effects it can have on a person with dwarfism. It's your hope that it will be published one day so it can raise awareness about dwarfism, and help educate the public on what it's like having dwarfism and living in a world not designed for you. Contrary to the popular childhood rhyme *Sticks and stones may break my bones but words will never hurt me*, words *do* hurt. Words have a lasting impact. Being called the 'm' word has stuck with you and brings up negative connotations from history. So you are careful what you say to people and are always kind.

Writing is your form of resistance and standing up for yourself and others. Last year you participated in a journalling workshop – a collaboration between Words of a Feather and The Provocative Inklings. The theme for the week was 'Finding Your Space'. One prompt was to think about a time in your life when you felt fierce and stood up for yourself, which gets you thinking about fierceness. The next was to write about a time when you had to learn to be gentle again. Your initial reaction was you're already gentle, so you reframed the question to 'How does writing make me fierce?' You wrote: *Writing makes me fierce because I can take on the persona of someone else. I can take on the persona of someone who's confident. I can take on the persona of someone who isn't afraid to stand up to others and isn't afraid of the consequences. Writing makes me fierce because I can share the things I'm too afraid to share out loud. Writing makes me fierce because it helps me affirm my opinions and beliefs and maybe, just maybe, it will give me the confidence to say them aloud.*

Writing is your resistance. Writing makes you fierce.

Marina Sano

Body

When you have lived your life led by mental illness and a fear of its return, whether in familiar shapes or new, how can you know what it feels like to be well? How can you know 'well' enough to realise how disabling this chronic illness and fear is? How can you know whether the 'well' that you are striving for is weighted by an ableist view of how to achieve it? Who is to blame if you've internalised this? How do you extricate yourself from all of this?

*

Historically, my solution to intersecting mental illnesses has been to forgo the thing that will help one if it will make the others worse. This makes sense on a practical level: it is an obvious act of self-preservation. Followed to a full conclusion, it is also technically 'self-care'. But everyone – the internet, the doctor, your friends, your family, people on the street in conversation, unprompted – will tell you how good moving your body is for you, how you need to get your endorphins pumping to help with the 'happy chemicals', how it's good for your heart health, and that they know it's hard when you're depressed but they promise, exercise really does help.

But when any exercise induces compulsive body checking, weighing your body, a scrutinising eye towards anything that you may consume, it feels a lot less like self-care. When every time you have been desperate enough to attempt *this* version of 'helping yourself', it has ended in a spiralling that takes the depression along with it for the ride. It has not felt like self-care. Every time you have felt that extra push in your body that tells you you may finally have the spare energy to expend on something other than the basic functions of life, the push has been coming from a separate illness that is sly and manipulative, that has been waiting for valid grounds to begin the cycle once more.

Eventually, I gave up on this notion of exercise as the thing I needed for my wellness. These people have not been navigating the same knot of illnesses as I have.

*

Recently, there has been a spark that feels unrelated to any illness, and it has given me extra energy in my body that feels like it could be spent, as we are told to think, *productively.* For the first time I can recall, my body is light. It is easy to move through the world. It is patient and available and, seemingly, *alive.*

The only tangle is that it has coincided with a time when I am aware the numbers have decreased and my body literally *is* a bit lighter than it has been in the last year. But who is to say anymore whether that is a factor when this time it really was incidental. This time, maybe it is just how my body is when it has this lightness to its step.

When your brain has not been entirely your own for as long as you can think back, it becomes impossible to truly delineate where the healthy thoughts begin and end, and where they are being directed by illness. But in this time when I feel as though my brain might be, at long last, my own – is this not the time to try? To set those habits that we are told *will do you a world of good!* The habits they say are *the building blocks of a healthy life.* To set in motion *looking after yourself* beyond swallowing the pills every morning.

Is this not the time?

*

It was $50 to try five exercise classes over a fortnight, using a machine I can't reasonably access for free. This breaks down to be about half the normal rate of their classes. I'd be a fool not to give it a go in this period of clarity.

I signed up for these classes on a whim induced by my bewilderment at this new feeling of wellness. Trying to get started before this new feeling dissipates, I squeezed into morning classes at a time when (as a self-employed freelancer), I would usually still be asleep or just barely conscious. This logistical difference in needing to pick myself up and be on the move once I woke already stirred more wonder at the 'wellness'. Suddenly, it was easy to be awake and paying attention earlier in the morning. Suddenly, I am not forcing a leaden body out of bed and into clothes and out the door.

After the first class, I *wanted* to be awake and moving. I *wanted* to start my day with activity. I wasn't afraid that it would sap all my reserves for the day – or week – because I learned that this time, that wasn't what would happen.

In the classes, there's a focus on feeling 'long and lean', of matching your breath to your movements, and of, generally, *minding your own business*. Take it at your own pace, try this variation for a challenge, try it this way to make it a bit easier. Listen to your body, you know it best.

I've never been in this sort of space with the capacity to actually follow these instructions. But now I can. I can focus on feeling my muscles stretch out and appreciate how nice it is to use them. I can focus on the form of my movements to match them up to what I'm being told to do. I can focus on trying to use the muscles I'm being told to use.

It seems so simple, but this has never been my experience. Every other time, my thoughts have been consumed by the mirrors, the other bodies around me, my spiralling thoughts on whatever anxious tangent they have caught on, the physical heaviness of my body making it so *difficult* to move as I'm being told.

After my first class, I was floating. I'd never had such ease of movement, nor been so (relatively) able to focus simply on myself in a room full of people.

After my second class, in the midst of a work-related crisis that had been snatched out of my control, I felt this difference embodied. Everything I'd been so elated to experience the first time was there, but it was battling with a consistent crushing of anxiety over the situation. As soon as I left the class, I crossed the road and made a call to start resolving it, so I could snatch back my 'wellness' from where it was being sapped – and it *worked.*

My next classes took me back closer to the high of what I'd learned this activity could be for me. A focus on feeling long and lean, on engaging my muscles to see what they can do, feeling strengthened and awakened after I finish. Feeling like I have finally achieved what I've been told for all these years, the things that exercise will do for you and your mental health.

But I'm also starting to arrive later to avoid the feeling of presence in a room of strangers in the ten minutes between the door opening and instruction beginning. I'm waiting to go to the toilet until I arrive so I can go there and use up another minute or two. I'm taking an empty water bottle to know that I will have an excuse to loiter as I refill it there. I'm slipping into the room once it's almost full so I can just select an empty machine and pretend I'm stretching while I try to stop feeling so bodily conscious until instruction begins and I can turn inwards.

*

After two weeks, I can feel the difference in my body. Over a decade of only moving my body incidentally has left me weak in most areas, apart from the muscles one needs to get around and to lift reasonably heavy boxes regularly. These muscles are all newly strengthened.

I think.

Probably?

There's a pride to the firmness I can feel now when I poke at my newly cultivated muscles. A usefulness and a reassurance in this marker of 'good health'. But there's also a consciousness to it. I can track each small change. I don't mean to, but I find myself in front of mirrors more, on the scales, looking down at myself, searching for changes to notice. For differences. Upgrades. For what this whole exercise thing has done to my body, and if it's delivering on its promised aesthetic perks.

I'm also aware that it's only been two weeks. A far shorter period than one is typically told light exercise will yield any of these results. And yet I'm convinced that there has been change. These muscles have been largely neglected and my body has always been thin. It's not entirely unreasonable to think this combination would allow for slight physical changes to become apparent in this short period of time.

But this focus inwards brings me back to the old problem of mistrusting my perception. I cannot reliably know whether this change is truly apparent, or if it has been constructed by illness. Whether it is real and tangible, or if it is only my illness-led hyperawareness of my body that reveals these changes to me – or if these same thoughts have simply constructed a false perception of what I've come to think of as physical markers of health and with it, thinness.

Mired by this doubt, I ask my partner to confirm if I am engaging realistically with my body. He begrudgingly admits that the muscles I'm trying to show him feel a little firmer, but more than that, his response is an expression of concern. He explains that you can't develop big changes in two weeks. I tell him I know that, *but see, my thigh is* hard*!*

Technically, we're both right. But this experiment just brings me back to the initial question: is engaging in exercise in this way actually healthy for someone like me? Is my claim that I want to improve my cardiovascular health so it more closely resembles my actual age and not someone much older just a lie I am telling myself? Do I actually care about having stronger muscles outside of the firmness they will bring? Am I going to eat in a way that compensates for this increased activity, no matter how light it may be? Or are these all lies I have constructed for myself to distract from a motivating thought that underlies my decisions? Of striving for thinness?

*

The thing about having had an eating disorder is that as recovered as one becomes, the thought patterns are something you can always recognise. When they begin to creep in seemingly of their own accord, if you wait a few months or even a few years, it turns out that your disordered thoughts making themselves known again was actually just the canary in the coalmine for a broader cultural return to thinness as a marker of superiority.

When your experience of the eating disorder – as it commonly is – has been enmeshed with anxiety, depression, and neurodivergence, how can you possibly decipher when the actions you take to heal one illness (or in the case of neurodivergence, an accommodation you make for yourself) is causing one of the others to flare back into illness and disability? When your illness has been a part of your thought processes for as long as you can remember, how are you to tell when you are experiencing healthy, non-illness-motivated thoughts and growth, as opposed to a change that to others is positive, but to you is being enabled by a filtration of deception? How can you trust your own mind when you know you've had these thoughts before, but the difference between it being illness and not is the motivation and eventual outcome?

How do you play the long game with your mind when, if you choose the wrong team, you will die? Perhaps if you're lucky, it will stop at the point where you just *want* to die. Or perhaps you will end up trapped in the cycle again, powering through the illnesses lest you stop and be caught in this death spiral.

No-one knows your body as well as you do.

Mario Licón Cabrera

Approaching blindness

(A sequence)

How dark the boundary of light
where nothing
reappears

– Jorge Valente

1
Allow the guava's aroma
to invade your place and let its aroma
remind you of the colour of its skin of light.
Yellow-pink light, like the desert's light at sunset.
Now that light fades away
from your eyes.

2
There is no face in the mirror.
In the mirror there are only moving
spots, dots, colours and lines. And all that
exists only inside your eyes—
and all that causes you nausea and doesn't allow you to see
your face in the mirror.

3

The black spot in the centre
of your eyes grows, like thick fog. And
that dense, dark fog threatens to cover
every single thing around the twilight
        of your gaze.

4

Zaz! This fulminant Autumn Sun
strikes your forehead as it sets
and blinds you completely making you see
what doesn't exist.
And though fearful, my steps
go ahead, stubborn, amongst obstacles and monstrous
shadows that don't exist.
To stroll facing Autumn sunset
is to reach a luminous precipice.

5

Attempting to stare at
the others' faces
only increases the diameter and thickness
of that ominous black spot that erases
all their details.

6

To hear and not to see. To hear
the atrocious squawk and not to see
neither colour nor shape
of that bird, alarmingly calling.

7

There you go, alone
all along the dark street amidst
an endless parade of swift faceless silhouettes.
The cars' lights blind you even more.

8

Suddenly, for an instant
light is made: on the walls
the sun multiplies the windows.

9

Deep inside your eyes the mist grows thicker.
The mist covers everything deep inside your eyes.
Outside, the roar of the sleepless children's screams
grows louder in your sombre neighbourhood.

10

Beyond the thick-dark talking silhouettes
        a thin ribbon of golden light reminds you of
the glorious Sonoran Desert sunsets of your youth—
when your eyes were still fully alive.

Kerri Shying

October and the old ones fly back home

there are others
singing their hearts out in the yard
today   bush people   orchids   bromeliads
strappy and glossy
the full tall galangal being the heart of the soups
up in the square garden
        which had a fallow year ready to be stripped out
        and planted with soybeans
        a staple of this space
        beside the dwarf Meyer lemon
a spotty cane begonia is flowering
in a candy-red so rich it looks like a lolly
the sugar bush
        that is for Rob Schackne
        coming on for first flowering
        oh boy, I knew he'd be keen
and the rope hoya of Gaagang's
a wreath   a beauty
now flowering in three gardens
as his cuttings flourish
here in memory
                I sketch a light watercolour of Max the dog on shiny
                    paper
                and on rag for my daily connection
                and now
                seated on the porch in the sun
                there's a bite to it
                we are not all growing old

sometimes I avoid taking care of myself
by throwing effort into work
rest   read
still waiting for the fucking ndis to decide
to fix the wheelchair

February
 in gimptopia   this morning
our yard being
a creature by itself
the scent of the loquat
that dream tree of all our grandmothers
 the native bees go to every small flower in turn
methodical and unhurried
 returning to a knothole in the porch post

sitting in the bliss
despite
new challenges of the colony
here is the lemongrass
the river mint for tea
ginger knuckles swollen underground for fish and tofu
pale lilac camphor laurel chatters with the frogs
leather finger limes with red centres
wait for me to pick them cack-handed
prickly   boot and glove time

I cook
 scouring the five treasures
rinsing off the starches
blister the capsicum from scarlet down to black
ingrain carbon   glaze my nails with garlic
strip that membrane between

vegetable and food
listen to the donabe sputter steam
blanch the cauli bake up
white to black ready
for the barramundi later

you are lingering
outside in that old laundry tub
of stainless steel
beside the Okinawa slow bolt shallots
ready to be the crunch in the roasted sweet potato mash
you know the good spots
a creak in the side gate wheels of your bicycle
patient with care
always art
our beloveds close and open flowers
as they go

TextaQueen

return

traffic through double glass
thrum of a world beyond
the return to normal
they're sold on a solid idea
relief is ahead
destinations on offer again
desired things ready to be found

outside is a world
determined to meet its end
inside we sit alone and take note

left behind   out of time
we continue to make time obsolete
voice notes skim oceans in an instant
first words i've spoken out loud today
DM Seen 3:14am
chain-smoking loneliness since 2020 <3
discord from ableds shared in an app
omfg i'd have a meltdown too
threads stitch us   together out-of-sync

group chat alert vibrates
somewhere under blankets pets pills
phone as hard to find as spoons
our connection untied to consistency
we send each other ease we wish to feel

our choirs meet on screens
wormholes to let us warble
        there is no path to light
    no A to B to Z
        no numbers will be called
    there is nothing to fail
        productivity is fake
    success is brief illusion

our harmonies fade out the hum
return us to each other
back to the disabled future

Notes

'spoons' as units measuring finite disabled capacity coined by Christine Miserandino in *The Spoon Theory*.

'productivity is fake' from a lutte collective poster and t-shirt design that reads 'time is not real/productivity is fake/what you produce doesn't matter'.

'back to the disabled future' alludes to Leah Lakshmi Piepzna-Samarasinha's book *The Future is Disabled*.

this flower has a spine

on my footpath i find a flower
it has a spine
moves like a centipede
thin black petal legs
encased in carbonite shell
blood of liquid copper
invisible to everyone but me

i pick it up
for my white polo buttonhole
fifty of one hundred legs
tickle my neck
we wriggle in my uniform

i carry it on the school bus
kids-a-tumble bubble
the melting pot
ready to liquefy me
my flower's cool felt feet
patter rhythms on my collarbone
we stay solid together

everyone underwatch in class
butts suction to plastic seats
my companion dares to free itself
scuttles across my desk
jumps around the room
past   teacher
                    chalkboard
          wall charts
slithering in the ears of every kid
learning how to be one

my clever friend returns to me
sits up on my shoulder
reports its research
whispering clicks and whistles
slides back inside my shirt

if only i understood its language

POEM: prescribed for the temporary relief of pain

care note: self harm

DIRECTIONS FOR USE

- Ball fist until nails break skin
    - place palm on margarita rim
    - salt the red crescents
    - savour the sting

- Bite inside of cheek hard
    - taste sweet metal seep
    - refuse ice if offered
    - wait for welt to form

- Outside club sit drunk in gutter
    - hit head against concrete
    - until someone intervenes
    - or skull cracks

- Drag kitchen knife against wrist
    - if too dull to draw blood
    - get some help
    - to sharpen the blade

- Run boiling bath to full
    - sink in without flinching
    - submerge with open eyes
    - see if you survive

CB Mako

No-one left behind

Calloused fingertips clasp around my classical music instrument's four-stringed fingerboard. The moment I sit on the local community orchestra's viola section, I am fifteen years old once again. Muscle memory slides into place.

Back straight, both feet firmly planted on the floor, I move my instrument in place. My viola slots perfectly with a detachable custom-made shoulder rest, on that space between left jaw, chin, and shoulder.

My facemask firmly in place as rehearsal begins.

I'm the only musician who continues to wear a facemask, five years into the pandemic.

After a whole evening rehearsing a variety of classical music for the community orchestra, I cycle away from the venue as the night deepens. I am mentally and physically exhausted when I reach our small, rented house.

*

Long Covid had dug deeper into microscopic places that mainstream doctors and medical specialists refuse to acknowledge. Like a thick, heavy white blanket, anything about Covid abruptly disappears. The coronavirus is not allowed in everyday conversations.

Many countries have moved on, while my slowly deteriorating body refuses to co-operate this fifth year of once-in-a-lifetime global pandemic.

Even the language about the pandemic changes, befitting the non-disabled, ableist society, who use the words 'post-Covid' even when the WHO said at the end of 2024 that:

> In the past five years, more than 7 million deaths from Covid-19 have been reported to WHO, but we estimate the true death toll to be at least three times higher. We cannot talk about Covid in the past tense. It's still with us, it still causes acute disease and 'long Covid', and it still kills.
>
> On average this year, about 1000 deaths from Covid-19 have been reported to WHO each week – and that's just from the few countries that are still reporting.
>
> The world might want to forget about Covid-19, but we cannot afford to.

*

The day after orchestra rehearsal, my body succumbs to post-exertional malaise (PEM), Postural Orthostatic Tachycardia Syndrome (POTS) and brain fog. My pre-existing medical conditions of diabetes, cardiovascular disease and asthma place me at higher risk for long Covid. I am mostly bedridden for the next two days.

This unfamiliar feeling of being unable to physically get out of bed, my muscles to my very bones refuse to budge as if I'm magnetised to the bed's mattress. Yet, I force myself, drag my unco-operative limbs and continue adulting and parenting my #LongCovidKids. I take a multitude of supplements to function for the day.

*

On 20 November 2022, I develop a very high fever due to Covid (which our entire household caught the week the state government removed all pandemic mandates in time for the state elections).

An unusual sound – a short snick, a crack, grinding crunch sound – unexpectedly occurred somewhere deep in the middle of my head, somewhere between my ears, deep behind my eyes. My chest felt heavy, like my 60-kilo offspring was sitting on me. My heart pounding so hard and loud, like I ran a marathon, while shivering from cold sweats. And for the first time, I cried like a five-year-old child, asking for my mum.

Soon, prescription medication Lagevrio arrived at our doorstep, a community delivery from our local chemist. Luckily, our asthmatic household had a standby nebuliser. A boxful of Pulmicort ampoules were delivered as well. Thank goodness for home deliveries.

*

Today is remote learning day for my immunocompromised, disabled child. She is unable to go to school every day since catching the deadly coronavirus. The calendar shows it is mid-2024. My child is regressing. The once-lively child now sleeps most of the day, and her therapists note significant tremors when she walks and when she writes. And just like me, she easily tires, runs out of breath, and succumbs to exhaustion.

Nowadays, she barely speaks and has resorted to gestures. Her medical team at the Royal Children's Hospital's new T21 clinic is in the process of assessing whether she has long Covid or Down Syndrome Regression Disorder. The waitlist to see multiple specialists – neurologist, otologist, paediatrician, and respiratory clinic – is long.

Our asthma management requires a nebuliser as puffers no longer work. Didn't they say children won't be affected by Covid? And yet, hashtag #LongCovidKids exist to this very day, fighting to be heard. The search for a cure continues.

*

In my fury, agony, and despair at the continuous gaslighting by the medical community and the non-disabled, I hold back my tears. A new genre of books is slowly building – all about disability, testaments of lived experience being disabled. I read these books and hold them dear, books authored and edited by people of colour:

Alice Wong, Leah Lakshmi Piepzna-Samarasinha, and Shayda Kafai to name a few.

However, most books published are by disabled white authors in (so-called) Australia. Disabled BIPOC/QTBIPOC writers are tokenised and pushed aside, prioritising the mainstream white narrative.

The CCTV snapshot of a white woman beating up an Asian woman in the early days of one of the many Covid lockdowns is burned into my memory. The intersection of racism and long Covid should be part of historical research around how non-white people were harassed the moment the once-in-a-lifetime pandemic began. To this very day, the loudest voices of disability, chronic illness, and long Covid are from the white mainstream. And yet they remain silent as we proudly wear 'Readers and Writers Against the Genocide' t-shirts, letting the complicit know that there cannot be disability justice without a 'Free Palestine!' According to the principles of disability justice, all of our struggles are connected, including our fight against ableism, racism and colonisation.

As disabled writer Dom Kelly wrote,

> Disability justice is rooted in principles of intersectionality, collective access, and cross-movement solidarity. It was founded by Black, brown, and queer disabled people who understood that liberation is either for everyone or it is for no one. That includes disabled Palestinians. That includes Gaza. That includes those disabled by bombings, by starvation, by blockade, by trauma. That includes every soul stolen from this world.

*

A 'Women's Covid-19 Capsule' is due to be unearthed in fifty years. Buried at the Queen Victoria Women's Centre on 12 March 2022 by curator Katie Sfetkidis, among the messages during an exhibition called 'Present/Memory', my message 'No-one Left Behind' was included in the time capsule. And yet, merely three years since the time capsule was buried, the immunocompromised, disabled, and those with chronic illness and long Covid are left behind.

*

As I write this piece, we are in the middle of winter, unable to turn on the house's ducted heating. Plunged into poverty due to the ongoing high-cost-of-living crisis and housing crisis. Our landlord has increased our rent so significantly, I need to make a choice whether to buy medication for long Covid or buy food for both my offspring. There is only room for one choice. I choose to feed my children first.

I cling to the hope that my grant application will be approved so I can continue to play my viola. The orchestra venue has moved farther from my suburb. Will I have the capacity to cycle at least fourteen kilometres each week for rehearsal?

Only time can tell how far my body will go. I cling to the hope for a cure either for myself or for both my children, the future generation of disabled advocates.

Hem Sid Chandran

As I see it

I am Autistic and a non-speaker. This essay describes my efforts to live my own life and make it rewarding.

My advocacy focuses on that segment of the Autistic population that is non-speaking. When I write or present about non-speakers, I am an advocate for all non-speakers and not just myself. I stand for others like me who don't use spoken language. That does not mean that we don't count or have anything to say. It just means that we have become invisible.

I belong to the not-so-rare breed of Autistics who use Augmentative and Alternative Communication (AAC). The alternative system I use is spelling words and sentences on a speech-generating device. Through AAC I am able to say, 'I am a non-speaker but not a non-thinker.' Through the use of an alternative communication system, I have gained self-respect. I now have a positive self-image.

I have an interest in the profoundly Autistic population. They have only recently received any attention from the scientific and research community. But I would like the general community to give us a place in the sun.

Many Autistic non-speakers would agree that our lives are like a seesaw. I'll explain what I mean. Sometimes I'm on top. At other times I hit rock bottom. I doubt that you would understand what I mean unless I go into details. Only another Autistic immobilised by apraxia, both motor and speech, will understand. We experience ups and downs, and both the ups and downs can be disconcerting to others and disabling to us. My sensory overload can cause a kind of delay and distortion in my perception resulting in mayhem. I am responding to the chaos I perceive but others don't see. My actions get dysregulated to a greater or lesser degree depending on how disturbed my perception is at that moment.

With the challenges that we Autistic non-speakers experience, living a full life is not easy. It takes a lot of work and determination. Autistics who do not speak have verbal apraxia. Many like me have generalised apraxia. Those of us who have generalised apraxia have difficulty looking after ourselves. This is a blow to our self-esteem.

Experiencing all of this, when I say I want to live a full and rewarding life, it can seem unrealistic. Working as a writer to record my experiences of a world that is seen through my lens is important to me. Writing is part of my advocacy, and I would like more opportunities to play an advocacy role in the community. I want to advance the cause of Autistic non-speakers. We are isolated and conquer challenges every single day. We struggle to meet and put our minds together to make change. Not many believe we have a mind. The media has no time for us.

Another aspect of living a full life is to have independence. To me, independence means that I ultimately have control of my life. It is important that others respect my wishes, even when they may not feel convinced that I am on the right track.

I want to be able to express my feelings more efficiently through my means of communication. To do this I need to be able to self-regulate. If you know severe Autism you will know how significant this is. Many of us cannot tell our bodies to do what we want. I have motor disturbances combined with sensory sensitivity which make it hard for me to compose myself to complete a task. I work every day trying to organise my body.

I look to AI to bring changes to how I use my speech-generating device. I think that having more options for my life will depend on learning about AI. I hope AI will help to design technology that will increase my independence, especially in communication. I want to be able to speak without the interface of a keyboard.

For me, travel is a big part of living a full life. I like travel for various reasons. I take pleasure in seeing a scene close up that I have seen depicted. I love to look at familiar monuments because they are famous and note the difference between the picture and the actual structure.

As well as giving priority to building independence in all aspects of life, pursuing my role as a writer and an advocate is essential to my sense of purpose. I have published a book titled *An Unspoken Story* describing my experience of living with Autism. I am working on my second book. In relation to my role as an advocate for non-speaking Autistics, I have done webinars and other presentations on how an AAC device can help one to advocate. I use an iPad with a speech-generating app.

Through my writing I would like to advocate for the independence that is so dear to those of us who are dependent on others in their everyday lives. You might ask what I mean by independence. To put it concretely I see it as:

Being able to go out on my own.

Managing my money.

Making friends.

Pursuing a career of my choice.

I hope that a time will soon come when I will be doing things that everyone else can. At this time, myself and people like me, can only hope for nominal autonomy. That is still something.

Note

Apraxia is when it is hard for you to move or gesture.

Ari Spanos

Being me, being Greek

Hi, I'm Ari. I use they/them pronouns. I'm neurodivergent (including Autistic and ADHD), disabled, mad, queer, genderqueer and intersex. You might think that's a lot of labels, and you're right. I've come to describe myself this way because these descriptors serve a helpful function for me.

Whenever our experience differs from the constructed social norm, discovering and claiming identities like these can help us understand and accept ourselves. I'm not the default; people will make incorrect assumptions about me until I prove them otherwise. It's important to me that people know who I am – using this language helps people 'get' me.

When writing that introduction, I realised that one descriptor I didn't use was 'Greek'. This is despite the fact that my grandparents all immigrated to Australia in their youth, my parents speak fluent Greek, and I grew up surrounded by Greek culture.

As a child I became very resistant to my Greek heritage. One funny example from when I was about ten comes to mind, when my cousins all wanted to watch *Grease*. I was vehemently against this movie choice until I was assured it wasn't, in fact, about the country.

As I've reflected over the years, I've developed some theories as to why I started rejecting my culture so early in my life:

Being dragged along to the Greek Orthodox Church, where we had to sit still and silent, listening to a drone of Ancient Greek hymns and choking on incense. We were made to stand in solemn vigil whether it was a wedding, christening or funeral. When I hit puberty, I learned that we weren't allowed to take Holy Communion when we were on our periods. Our bodies were too dirty to accept the blood and body of Christ. All this despite the fact that the meaning behind this bleeding, our capacity to give birth, was supposedly our single most essential function.

I was forced into Greek school, which for me meant sitting at an old lady's dining table after primary school with my sister and cousins. We were made to recite grammatical rules over and over for reasons that seemed pointless to me. I remember getting so frustrated once that I broke a pencil. My only respite was the biscuit break halfway through.

Within my family, there were strong ideas of who I should be. I could talk about the gender dynamics forever, but there was also a lot that impacted me from a disability perspective. Arriving at huge family events, having to kiss and make small talk with distant relatives who felt like strangers, and do it all over again when we left – it was an Autistic nightmare. As a young child I was known for bellowing 'OOOME' to my parents when I'd had enough at these overwhelming events. In retrospect, I'm surprised I coped as well as I did.

As I got older, my behaviour was swiftly corrected by the adults around me. My ways of being – sitting, moving, speaking – were improper and shameful. Part of my behaviour was just being a kid, and part of it was Autistic expression. As an Autistic person, I often express and regulate my emotions and internal state externally. This is commonly known as 'stimming' – I rock from side to side when I stand, I shake my hands when I'm excited or frustrated, I can be too loud or too quiet, I zone out into my own world.

But shaking your leg while sitting in the pews at church for hours is shameful. Speaking out of turn when your grandparents are lecturing you is disrespectful. Going against the grain in any way is a sure-fire way to disgrace your family and ensure you never win a respectable Greek husband.

The multitude of Greek weddings I've been to are the peak demonstration of this rhetoric. They're always huge affairs, filled with hundreds of distant relatives and other Greek revellers. Looking and behaving your best is essential – if not to win over a potential husband, then at least to avoid provoking never-ending gossip from the aunties who have nothing better to do. Whatever us kids do is a direct reflection on our parents, grandparents and our futures.

I'll never forget the night I refused to wear heels to one of these events. Heels are painful and uncomfortable for almost everyone. As an Autistic person, there are some additional downsides:

I am keenly aware of pain, and any discomfort I feel is usually an addition to the baseline discomfort I feel from the overwhelm of being in the world, let alone at a loud and crowded wedding.

I have challenges with motor co-ordination that come with being disabled.

I have a strong sense of justice, and baseline of constantly questioning social norms and expectations.

My teenage self resolutely stomped down the stairs in flats, to the disheartened and pleading faces of my mum, sister and aunt. I tried to reason with them – why should sore feet force me to sit down when everyone else is having fun cavorting in a circle? Isn't it such a blatant and straightforward example of sexism? But they remained firmly entrenched in their position – *'This Is Just the Way Things Are'.*

*

I wouldn't blame you for thinking that my goal here is to bemoan my family and culture. And truth be told, I do harbour a lot of resentment. But there's also a lot that I love about my culture: the focus on family and community, the interdependence and support we offer each other, the celebrations and the gregarious nature of them. These aspects of Greekness align with my values – community, mutual support, fun.

I've noticed Aussies can take more time to warm up to you. There's more of an initial social distance, more decorum. In Greek culture, you're welcomed generously with open arms – into our families, our homes, and to the (always excessive amounts of) food at our table. But there's a caveat to this – it's granted only if you are being a Proper Greek like they expect, or masking well enough to make it seem like you are.

I still have to consciously mask at family events, and the older (Greeker) the attendees, the more essential this charade. I am constantly aware of my body language, what I say and how I say it. Regardless of how I feel, to keep the peace I must ensure that I'm perceived as respectful, politely interested and ready to offer service. This takes a toll on all of us, but as it's so opposed to my natural Autistic ways of being, I leave these events feeling fatigued, frustrated and alienated.

*

I made the decision to change my name a few years ago. As a gender-diverse person, it was something I had been considering for a while. I asked some friends to start calling me Ari, and I liked it, so that's what I'm called now.

When I was born, I was given the name Maria. I was named after my grandmother, as is tradition in my family. If I'd have been born with a different set of genitals I would have been Nicholas – along with about five of my cousins.

I chose to change my name for a lot of reasons. Some of it had to do with gender, but more broadly it had to do with the fact that I couldn't reconcile the differences between 'Maria' and who I now understand myself to be. Let me explain.

I wasn't just assigned a gender at birth – I was assigned 'Maria', which came with an even narrower set of expectations than the female gender marker. 'Maria' would be a good little girl, friendly but not too loud, polite and petite. 'Maria' would grow up into a beautiful young woman, with interests that befitted a teenage girl – clothes, make-up, and nice Greek boys. 'Maria' should embrace the opportunities her grandparents afforded her by immigrating to Australia: get a good education, go to university, find a job that pays well. But all that would be secondary to 'Maria's' top priority – finding a husband and raising children.

Aside from the obvious – I didn't even meet their most basic expectation of growing up to be a woman – there's so much about 'Maria' that isn't true for me. It quickly became apparent that 'Maria's' destiny of marrying young and raising children wasn't the path I was on.

I am attracted to men – gender doesn't impact who I'm interested in. But when interacting with Greek men, I discovered that many of them hold these same expectations of Greek womanhood, at least to some extent. Expectations that have never made sense to me; I've long abandoned the notion that I could authentically or sustainably meet them.

When it comes to spending time with children, I enjoy the opportunity to unmask, be silly and unfiltered. I love my niece more than the world; I'm so grateful to share our special bond and watch her grow up. But I know I could never have kids of my own.

Autistic people can be, and are, incredible parents. But just speaking for me specifically, child rearing is not something I'm capable of. I have intense sensory sensitivities – to light, sound, smell, movement – things that kids create in abundant, overwhelming and diverse ways. I get tense and irritable quickly when I'm overstimulated, and can lash out if I'm not able to accommodate my needs in those moments. It's not an anger management issue – my brain and body will always be intensely activated by these stimuli. Once I learned that I'm Autistic, I was able to start learning about, accepting and accommodating my needs rather than trying (and failing) to change how my brain works.

Being Autistic and ADHD disables me in this society. I say this in terms of the social model of disability: viewing disability as a result of societal and environmental barriers, rather than individual impairments.

My constant fatigue, executive functioning challenges, and the added energetic cost of daily tasks mean I can't work a full-time job, nor take care of my personal needs independently while working. I am incredibly grateful and fortunate to have both family and formal supports to accommodate this.

This all ultimately means I have chosen not to have children – which isn't a problem for me. The idea of having that level of responsibility for another human being(s) leaves me feeling trapped and terrified. A lot of the time even just being responsible for myself feels overwhelming.

I'm grateful that our big Greek family culture facilitates me being a big part of my niece's life. Unfortunately, no matter how joyful, fulfilling and meaningful my life ends up being, I know I'll always be seen by my family as having failed by not having children. Their narrative will be that I never got chosen by a good man, that I'm cursed to live out my days lonely and ashamed. And if all goes as it should, all the people I need to convince otherwise will be long gone before I can prove that I can die happy and child-free.

*

On the other hand, it's important to acknowledge that, at times, my Greek family culture has been my saving grace. I am currently twenty-nine years old and living with my parents. I tried moving out a few years ago, but it only lasted a few months before it became clear that I wasn't coping. That experience was the start of me realising that I'm disabled. But when I came home, feeling defeated and ashamed, my parents welcomed me back with open arms.

To them family is everything, which means I can continue to live with and be supported by them until I establish what I need to live out of home. I know many Australian families have the opposite response: hoping kids will move out as soon as they turn eighteen or making them pay board as soon as they get a job. I honestly don't know what I would have done in those circumstances, as a young disabled person who didn't know they were disabled. I don't disparage this approach – it's just a big cultural difference.

Despite acknowledging the aspects of my culture that I love and benefit from, I'm still not 'Maria'. I could have reclaimed the name, redefined what it means to be 'Maria'. But honestly, I have to hide so much of myself from my family that it ultimately seems redundant. Ari fits better. Ari is part of the language I've learned to understand and accept why I'm not 'Maria' – neurodivergent, disabled, mad, queer, genderqueer and intersex. Most of my family don't know any of this about me, and so they don't know me as Ari. To them I'm still 'Maria'.

Maybe that's why I don't use 'Greek' to describe myself. It's assumed. Or if not, I've never been made to feel like I should be any different. I've never experienced discrimination or xenophobia based on my heritage, but my parents and grandparents have. Maybe that's why they're so proud to be Greek. This feels like a breakthrough.

*

When I reflect on my life experience from this lens, I consider my ancestors.

Not that far back, just a few generations ago, my family was living so differently. There must have been people like me in my family tree. But what did someone like me do on the tiny Greek island of Kalymnos? How did they reconcile their differences from what was expected of them? Without the language, social and cultural context that I have, where did that leave their identity?

The most obvious answer seems to be: they probably masked into the person they were expected to be their entire lives. Women needed to get married, have kids and be homemakers. Perhaps they might have been viewed as a bit eccentric, 'the village crazy lady', but this standard life path was inevitable. Because they had nowhere to go. Literally, locked in by water. No options, no alternatives were available to them.

Their stimming or otherwise odd ways of behaving, if they couldn't hide them, would have been more than frowned upon or reprimanded. They might have faced religious intervention. This isn't hyperbole – a friend of mine's mum was subjected to an exorcism in Greece, facilitated by her family, because she has epilepsy.

I wonder how their disability would have been interpreted. Would they have been seen as 'bad wife material', shunned and shamed forever to be a spinster? Or would they have been married off before anyone noticed their limitations, then doomed to never live up to their role as perfect mother and wife?

Or could they have been less disabled on that tiny island? Could those traditional gender roles I so bemoan have worked in their favour? If they weren't expected to work, would they have had the capacity to maintain a home and raise children? Would being presented with a single clear, simple path in life have worked well for their Autistic brain? Without other options available to them, could they have been a happy and fulfilled wife? If they were struggling, would the culture of interdependence, the literal 'village', have stepped in to help them raise their children?

Because that's the thing about Australia – the ongoing impacts of colonialism mean we're hyper-individualistic, living under an illusion of meritocracy and something about bootstraps. At its most extreme, an individual is seen as the cause of all their personal problems and the sole person who can, and should, resolve them all.

Growing up in Australia, I internalised many harmful myths: living with your parents at twenty-nine is 'lazy', embarrassing and behind. Leaning on friends and community for support is asking too much, co-dependent and intrusive. Being supported by the government is a waste of taxpayer dollars and if you just tried hard enough, you'd force yourself out of disability.

In this culture, we're siloed so thoroughly that it ends up being completely nonsensical. The first domestic homes were built without kitchens, because cooking was still such a communal activity. Why were my three housemates and I fighting over cooking space to make three separate dinners when it makes so much more sense to share the responsibility? Why does every house on the street have its own lawnmower, when it's something each household only needs for a few hours a week at most? Why are there so few spaces where people can gather and connect with community, without the expectation of spending money?

I'm going to end this line of questioning here. There are more informed people who write more eloquently on these subjects.

*

I've spent a lot of time feeling completely at odds with my cultural background – *they don't get me, they don't accept me.* These thoughts are valid and true.

But I'm starting to consider a second, parallel truth: there are aspects of my culture that are authentic to me in ways I didn't realise. And I might be able to claim these elements of Greekness and leave the rest behind.

When I accept and accommodate the needs of someone who might be considered 'lazy' by the broader culture, is that my Greekness? Is it my Greekness that helps me extend that same generosity to myself in accepting that I'm disabled? Is my Greekness why, despite the inaccessibility of living in Sydney, I could never see myself moving away from the friends and community I value so dearly?

Maybe I can start taking more pride in my culture. Not because I've been made to feel ashamed about it, but because I've been made to feel ashamed within it. Maybe it's time for me to reclaim the parts of Greekness that actually *affirm* my existence: leaning into my generous spirit, being community- and family-oriented and forever celebratory. Maybe being me and being Greek aren't mutually exclusive.

Franklyn Hudson

I am certain terrible things are going to happen to me

Once upon a time.

There was a child who wanted to be a knight. Ever since they can remember they have wanted to be able to slay monsters.

I am certain that terrible things are going to happen to me. So, I try to be in control of it. I count to seven, to twelve, every time I touch something as if that is going to reorient the centre of the universe to somewhere safe. I am trying to get the vibes of the universe in alignment with the feeling of tightness in my chest. I am trying to make it settle and trying to figure out how to breathe.

I like to vanish. Sometimes the world gets so loud that I have to tune it out. I disappear into my head, and I tell myself stories, and if I am there then I am not here.

I am a storyteller by trade. I want to be an author, and I have published at least one piece, so I count myself as a writer. Stories are where I run to when the world gets too hard.

Writing like this is leaving myself exposed, like a weeping open wound. But I can't tell if it is the fiction or the fact that opens it more.

Every day they get up and swing their sword at a tree trunk, undoubtedly blunting it, but this sword will never see a real fight, and they must hone their skill against something. To learn somehow, while they wait to hold the sword they will fight with.

Some days my anxiety is so bad that I cannot get off the couch. I curl up there under a mountain of blankets and try to disappear into stories. I read. I watch TV, I write. My head gets so loud, and everything is so hard, I cannot touch anything, seven, twelve, fourteen. I cannot eat anything; bringing foods into my house means that bad things will happen, no I can't tell you what they will be, just that I am sure of it.

The jousting tournament is today and it's the annual chance for the citizens of the realm to prove themselves to the king, and if they win it maybe even get knighted. It's the only thing they've dreamed of their whole life. They pull on their armour, scavenged from what no longer fits the soldiers and knights of their town. Of course, it is clunky and doesn't fit right.

Until I moved out of home I spent most nights on the floor of my parents' bedroom.

It is by no means a comfortable place to sleep and perhaps the fact that I can now sleep anywhere is because of all those nights that I spent sleeping there.

Even now when I go home, sometimes I find myself crawling upstairs to sleep near my parents, though these days I have migrated to the couch near their room rather than the floor.

I have probably spent more nights sleeping in their room than I have spent sleeping alone.

Recently my father reminded me that daylight savings was about to end, which meant I would get another hour of sleep. I realised for the first time that the rise of anxiety in my chest whenever I hear about daylight savings comes from the nights I spent terrified, as that hour ticked backwards and I had to relive the worst moments of my life over and over again.

I am not scared of the dark – but I am scared of the night.

I learnt to fall asleep to imaginary worlds.

The arena is a sacred space and they have never stepped in here before. This is the providence of knights and squires and those who have been permitted to hold swords. This is a space of power, and they want to be a part of it almost as much as they want to tear it all down.

The world has always been scarier than I have known how to handle. It's weird because I have never been afraid of the monster under my bed. In fact I used to hope there was a monster. I used to watch *Monsters Inc.*, and I hoped that my door would open and reveal a monster behind it.

I think that a real monster would have been easier. Would be easier.

Their first competitor steps into the arena across from them, and their training kicks in. It is nothing like a real fight, but it is something to lean on and as they parry blow after blow, they realise that they are stronger than they have given themselves credit for.

They tear down one man after another. Every sword blow a boost in confidence, slicing and stabbing in perfect rhythm. It is a dance that they have learnt, and they nail the steps perfectly.

My anxiety is not just something that lives in my head. It is a physical sensation that curls around my body like a snake and squeezes. I am scared all the time.

I am scared that something bad is going to happen to my body. That it is going to fall apart, and I will be powerless to stop it. That it will just give in, and it will mean that I will never be able to achieve my dreams.

It has already stalled me once. Something that I wanted more than anything fell through the cracks created by my anxiety. Now I am left in a tailspin, not sure where to go next because I worked so hard for it, and my anxiety took it from me.

The worst part is that saying that feels like an excuse, even if I know deep down that it is true. I pushed myself to my limits because I had to, to keep up with everyone else, and at the last hurdle my body betrayed me. I spent a year unable to keep up, tired and shattered, and now six years of work are down the drain, because I was fighting a war on two fronts and I lost.

I am so angry and sad all the time now. But more than anything I feel betrayed. I needed my body to work, and it didn't. It doesn't matter that I did the best I could because the truth is that it will never be enough.

In my head I could have done it.

They are bloodied and bruised. The blood is trickling down the side of their face, but they are triumphant as they stand in front of the king, a slew of bodies in their wake. This competition has changed them, something has happened in this arena, they have grown stronger, surer of themselves, and surer of what they must do now. They stepped into this arena with one goal in mind, but somewhere along the way they realised that it wasn't enough. That the men they slew to get here are meaningless if this all happens again. If every year this arena flows with the blood of those who fight in it, and if every year they have to come back and fight for their place. That's not what winning looks like.

The king stands in front of them, holding out his hand for their sword so that he can knight them. But if they hand it over, they become a soldier in his army and they have to fight for him every day, never escaping from his control.

That's not what they want.

That's not why they wanted to be a knight.

It's hard when you realise that the way to save yourself is nothing like you imagined it would be.

So they take a deep breath, and instead of handing over the sword, in one quick, deft movement, they pierce it through the king's chest. Shock fills his face; his expression stills and gets stuck with wide eyes and an open mouth as he clatters backwards and slams onto the ground.

It's a victory, but it had a cost.

In my imagination I get to conquer my anxiety. In my imagination I get to win.

That's not what real life looks like.

In the real world I still can't sleep through the night.

In the real world, I'm still fighting the eating disorder I've developed because all the food in the grocery store is cursed, and I can't bring it inside the house.

In the real world my chest is still tight all the time, my body shakes. I can't control the way my muscles are always tight, and my body is filled with an anxiety that tells me that any minute I'm going to have to fight for my life.

It's no wonder I wish the fight were tangible, something I could take a sword to and slay.

It's no wonder I'm a storyteller.

Skye Cusack

Here's what I think happened

Sometimes, if they're feeling confident enough, people will ask me if my dissociative amnesia is caused by a horrific childhood trauma. I'd love to tell them, but that's the thing about amnesia – I don't remember.

This is supposed to be a non-fiction anthology, but unfortunately due to the nature of my amnesia, some of these things might involve fabrication. I know, I know, but don't take it up with me. I'm going to forget I even wrote this by the time the book comes out.

You're allowed to laugh when you read this piece. I do. Several practical academic models have found humour is an effective way to reduce psychological stress, which I apparently have much of, so you have my full permission to cackle and guffaw to your heart's content. If you don't laugh, you cry, right?

So, without further ado, here's what I think happened during the loudest of times:

Things were mostly fine until I turned seventeen. I loved school, worked a couple of jobs to help support my family, and hung out with friends during my time off. I was living a pretty decent life for a teenager stuck in Tasmania.

Then, in Grade 12 ... something happened. There's a lot of debate in the clinical psychology field about the legitimacy of recovering repressed memories, and I'm not a psychologist, but with all my mental health presentations I've found an alternative path into the field.

My memory of that night changes every time I try to recall it. Since the worst-case scenario involves accusing someone of a serious crime, I'll try to speak with a little class. There was some touching, and sometimes I remember it all going very smoothly and consensually.

Most of the time I do not. But, honestly, I just don't know what happened.

All I know is, after that night, my entire life changed. Everyone close to me agrees that regardless of what exactly happened, from the next day onwards I just wasn't Skye Cusack anymore. I was this weird, hazy version of myself, like rolls of fog avalanching by way of a mountain, undulating downward.

The thing about trauma is that the only people you can ask for clarification are the people who were involved. In my case, the only one I could ask was the person I would report to the police if they admitted anything. I'm sure you can imagine how that would go:

I'd say, 'Hey, did you assault me?'

They'd say, 'No.'

I'd say, 'Yeah, of course. I'm sure my weird memory lapses are from 5G in the wi-fi or whatever.'

I went to the police. Well, a police officer that was stationed at a place in my community I visited often. He was a white, male cop who I heard later was friends with the family of the person I told him about.

To clarify, I did not report this person to the police. I just had a word with a police officer. Or, rather, I got two sentences out before *he* had a word with *me*.

He made it pretty clear that there was no point pursuing anything. He said that I was a less-than-average-looking Aboriginal girl who was known for being crazy. He was right about that – at the time, I was struggling with undiagnosed dissociative amnesia, OCD and bulimia.

He said that even if I could somehow pull myself together, he knew my family didn't have money, so I should drop it and just go home.

At the time, words like 'racist', 'ableist' and 'classist' didn't come to my mind. *Nothing* really came to my mind. I just accepted defeat and went into this beautiful place inside my head. I'd run away to this waterfall at the back of Burnie Park, just like I did as a kid in real life. Leaves would crunch underneath the soles of my second-hand jelly shoes as I leaned down and stared into the mosaic-tiled bottom of the waterfall. There were birds and bugs and I was never alone.

Sometimes the rushing of the waterfall would slow down enough for me to walk through. I'd pop out occasionally to find myself in the middle of a shift, or at a random party at some person's house, but mostly I stayed tucked away in this tiny pocket independent from mental consciousness.

It was more inconvenient than anything. Whenever I came back and realised three weeks had passed, I had to go get another STI test. I always came up clean, so that's one ray of light to shine on the dumpster fire that was this era of my life.

All the big things were covered, like working and going to school. Sure, I missed a few shifts and classes here and there, but for the most part everything was business as usual. I don't know how. I guess not even dissociative amnesia trumps capitalism.

It was the little things that I was losing. My ID, my keys, my wallet. It happened all the time, but I'm a fixer, so eventually I became better at finding things than losing them. Until one day at school, when I could not for the life of me find my phone.

Since I was so good at searching for things, I thought it might have been stolen. Just in case, I reported it as such by submitting a form to the Tasmanian police. The phone was cheap, so I just decided to cut my losses and get a replacement.

Then, to no one's surprise, I forgot all about this whole thing.

Life went on. I came to the conclusion that I'd probably made it all up anyway. How could I know what was real and what wasn't? We're meant to be a nesting doll of parts, a brain inside a skeleton inside flesh, but my consciousness wasn't at the centre like it was supposed to be. My daily experience was nothing but a series of clicks. Work, school, friends, nothing, work, school, friends, nothing, work, school—

Six months later, the police showed up on my doorstep. They didn't put me in handcuffs, but they did tell me to get into the police car and asked Mum to follow behind us in her vehicle.

White-hot terror. I wasn't used to feeling any inner sensations back then, my brain immediately shutting off when things got too intense, but in that moment I felt everything. Fear, confusion, guilt. The guilt was premature, because as they escorted me to their car they'd neglected to tell me what I had done.

I'd lost so much time in the last six months. My mind rushed straight to the worst possible scenario. Had I killed someone? Maimed them? Repeated the potential cycle and assaulted someone myself? The world of possibilities spiralled through me and punched out my core like an apple slinky machine.

I don't remember much after that, because the second they put their hands on me I left my body. I assume I sat quietly in the back while they drove. Maybe there was music on the radio. We might have made small talk. I know I didn't cry. I couldn't reach the tears inside me back then. They were too far buried under the fog. Besides, all the liquid had to stay inside my head to sustain the waterfall.

Once we arrived at the police station, I was taken into a room. I think it was quite dark and probably used for questioning suspicious-looking people like myself. Back then I had thick black eyeliner I'd learned from the best of the best on YouTube and a choppy side fringe I'd sliced with a Gillette razor blade. I walked into that room with Mum thinking, *by the time I leave this room again I'll know if I'm a murderer.*

If I had killed someone I would be really angry at myself for contributing to the stigma that people with dissociative disorders are violent. Look, I love James McAvoy more than most, but films like *Split* didn't do the dissociative disorder community any favours.

If I had killed someone, there was a special place in hell for M Night Shyamalan and me. We could spend a fiery eternity together, justifying our biggest mistakes in hopes of redemption: him, *Glass*; me, the eyeliner.

I can only remember flashes of the words we exchanged in that room. Before the conversation began, they started recording. They stated the time and their names and then asked me to state my name.

Then, in this serious situation taking place in a dark interrogation room, my mother sitting sombre beside me, I responded with a whine. 'Ugh, do I have to say my middle name? Because I hate it.'

I cringe every time I think about this. I'd like to submit that memory to my amnesia for consideration.

I stated my full name – middle name included – and then finally we started getting to the jam-filled centre of the 'donut situation' I'd found myself in. What's that, you ask? A situation you donut want to be in.

Okay, that pun was so lame I feel it would be justified to report me to law enforcement again.

These police were much nicer than the one I spoke to six months before, but I was still nervous because statistically, Aboriginal youth aren't treated particularly well in custody. Particularly in north-west Tasmania where I could have been sent to Ashley Youth Detention Centre, referred to as a 'child torture chamber' by the Tasmanian Aboriginal Centre in 2025 (after the horrific allegations of physical and sexual abuse against minors in custody).

I was expecting a tirade of questions about my alibi for a brutal murder, but instead they asked me about the police report I submitted for my lost phone. I relaxed. I wasn't in trouble.

Except ... surprise plot twist: they said they had video footage of me calmly walking up to a rubbish bin and dropping my phone in. It was so absurd that I wanted to laugh.

Maybe laughter wouldn't be most people's first reaction, but this was funny because it wasn't my first time getting in trouble for binning something.

When I was in Grade 1, I bought an icy pole from the school canteen and was given five cents change. I didn't have much need for a single five-cent coin, so I threw it in the bin. A teacher caught me and then – I kid you not – I got given a one-day suspension.

At six years old. For throwing five cents in the bin.

Maybe I'm still bonkers, but I don't think either of these things justified a suspension or questioning by the police. Hence, the absurdism.

I learn that it's actually not funny. I'm in trouble because I've submitted a false police report. They want me to go to some sort of junior tribunal – I can't remember what this was exactly, but Google has told me there is something in Tasmania for minors called a Community Conference, so maybe it was that?

A couple of months went by, me going in and out of the waterfall as I waited for the date and time of my next meeting. I wanted it over and I also hoped it never happened, because that's where they would decide on what my punishment would be.

I don't know where this falls in the timeline, but sometime during all of this I was accepted into the Aboriginal Centre for the Performing Arts in Brisbane. My local newspaper ran a story about it, with a big picture of my face accompanying the article.

None of it felt real. I had achieved my dream of getting into a performing arts school, but I was also probably about to be arrested or executed or whatever happens to Aboriginal underager ragers. It was too much for me. I had dropped out of school at this point and was working three jobs.

I was on the bus to a shift at KFC when I got a call from a very professional-sounding woman wanting to organise a time for my tribunal/Community Conference/death sentencing/whatever.

I was about two stops away, so I asked if I could call back to discuss after my shift. She said sure, and then I have no memory of anything between hanging up and the meeting I'm assuming I called her back to organise.

I had been expecting a very scary, official meeting in a courtroom. Instead, it was five people sitting in a room at the community house down the road from me. In the room with me was my mum, the lady I spoke to on the phone, a female social worker, and ... the cop who hadn't believed me at the beginning of all this.

I didn't like that he was there. It made me feel like this conversation was rigged. He had already proved that he thought I was bonkers and I knew he would see the worst of me. When it was his turn to speak, he insisted that I had submitted a false police report for attention and pushed for me to be charged.

The social worker had baked brownies or lemon squares or something and I ate them in a daze. I was really, *really* fucking scared. I hadn't knowingly submitted a false report. I genuinely still have no memory of throwing my phone in the bin. To this day, no-one has ever even showed me the footage.

Mum spoke next and testified that I was a dissociated legend, who often came home at 3 am covered in mud with no recollection of wandering around all night. I also had a letter from a clinical psychologist that validated my dissociative disorder diagnosis.

I don't know if the other woman there, the one who I had spoken with on the phone, was also a cop, or a facilitator, or a judge. All I know is that she got to make the decision about what happened to me. She listened to everyone and then said her piece, while my stomach bubbled up through my throat with fear.

The somehow-important woman agreed that I had submitted a false police report for attention, but said she wasn't going to ruin my future over it. She had seen me in the paper and was also very impressed when I told her I had a job. I had a *bright future ahead of me* and she didn't want one moment of attention-seeking to ruin it for me.

I mean ... I guess it was the second-best-case scenario? Sure, none of these people had believed me, but there was no charge, no community service, not even a fine. The only thing I got was free baked goods from the social worker. I went home and, for the first time in a very long time, I cried ... and cried ... and cried.

This is the weirdest sentence of my life, but I truly think working at KFC saved me. I wonder, what if I didn't have a job or hadn't been in the paper? Would it have made a difference? What would they have thought of me – an unemployed, mentally ill Aboriginal teenager living in a low socio-economic area in Tasmania? What about people who were in my situation who couldn't work, or didn't have access to a clinical psychologist? What would have happened to them?

Then I realised, I was investigated more for having a reaction to an alleged assault than the person who I tried to accuse. I was taken in a police car to the station, questioned, then sent to a community house to discuss whether or not I would be charged.

And the whole time they were, what, attending classes that I had to drop out of?

Maybe nothing happened. I genuinely don't know. I won't ever know. But I do wish there was at least some sort of investigation.

I lasted two months at the performing arts school before I came back to Tasmania and was submitted to the Northside Mental Health Unit. I wasn't fit for the real world, not back then. The only thing I could stand to look at was the texture of the waterfall smashing against the tiled ground beneath it. I did lots of therapy and eventually, I got better.

I don't know what the big message of this is. I guess if anyone finds themselves in a similar situation, make sure you're in your local newspaper so the legal system finds some semblance of respect for you?

My every attempt at justice, or even answers, was blocked by the brick wall of judgement. The only reason I am stable and well today is because of my grassroots community and my self-determination.

So, maybe the actual lesson I learned is to not go to the police at all. If I'd never had that yarn, never submitted that report, I could have been allowed to throw things in the bin in peace. Instead, I was over-questioned and under-heard until I ended up painting paper cups in a psych ward.

At least, that's what I think happened, anyway.

Carly-Jay Metcalfe

The colour of air

> Every sickness has an alien quality, a feeling of invasion and loss of control that is evident in the language we use about it.
>
> – Siri Hustvedt, *The Shaking Woman or a History of My Nerves*

31 December 2023

In the end, it's curiosity – and a little slip of vanity – that proves to be my undoing. I'm searching for a new perfume to buy for my birthday, so with my mask lowered, I diffuse the fragrance onto my radial pulse, then onto strips of cardboard. Later, I settle on the theory that it was the communal coffee beans that had been lying in wait for someone just like me.

For weeks, my gut had been cinching with a familiar knot of terror – the east coast of Australia was heaving with a fresh swell of Covid, and as the year rolled into 2024 it felt like I was tempting fate when I wrote in my notebook, *'I am still a "Novid"'*.

3 January 2024

On the second day of January, my throat feels scratchy – like a half-chewed potato chip has lodged in my windpipe – so I do a rapid antigen test. Negative. Around midnight, I'm woken up by violent rigours. Delirious, I don't have the capacity to call anyone because I am hyper-focused on regaining some semblance of warmth. It takes half an hour to work up the mental fortitude to switch my air conditioner to heat mode, pressing the button until it reaches 30 degrees. I have to steel myself to leave the warm refuge of my bed to search for a jumper, and by the time I've thrown up over the constellation of terrazzo that is my bathroom floor, I am too deep in delirium to recognise that what I'm bringing up is lime-green bile. It feels like someone has reached into my stomach and turned it inside out with a grip hook.

*

Just after 7 am, I call Dad.

'I think I'm sick. Like, Covid sick.'

'Oh no, love.'

'Just let me get some things together, then we can go to the hospital.'

Mum would ask me later, 'Why didn't you call us earlier?', which felt like an interrogation (it wasn't). I told her the only thing I could think about was getting warm.

I pack a bag at a lumbering pace and somehow find the mental acuity to throw in two books, some medication, underwear, my toothbrush, some clothes and warm socks. It takes me an hour to place these things into my Mary Poppins carpetbag as my dog gently pads around the house. She knows the carpetbag to be the harbinger of my impending departure. She tilts her head, both piqued and alarmed at my shaking body. The photos atop my grandmother's pianola jounce around as though more alive than me. Before Dad picks me up, I grab a disposable vomit bag from a bathroom drawer and burrow my face into the mouth of it for the drive to hospital.

I arrive at emergency and forget to check in because I'm feverish and everything feels as though it's moving at half-speed. I eventually shuffle over to triage where I tell a despondent nurse that I'm a lung transplant recipient and that I'm feeling unwell. Her eyes widen as she flounders about for a thermometer, which she pokes into my ear. Thirty-nine point seven degrees. I am quickly ushered through the doors and into the inner sanctum of the emergency department. I do not know it then, but I am in septic shock and acute adrenal collapse. Not long after I arrive, I'm shuttled down the hallway into a resuscitation bay due to my low blood pressure that will soon be incompatible with life. Very quickly, I feel a searing pain across my head. It stretches temple-to-temple, then colonises my entire skull, and every time I move, cough, or speak, it's like a kick drum being double-pedalled into my head. Delirium does not augur well, and yet I feel a sense of safety – possibly because my now-warm body is a mountain of blankets from the hot box.

In the resus bay, I hear a familiar script – 'This is Carly Metcalfe. Cystic Fibrosis, double lung transplant recipient of twenty-six years. She's come in with rigours and is hypotensive. We've done a PCR and are just waiting for those results. IV access is extremely poor.'

Being so dangerously hypotensive, I'm given multiple doses of adrenaline. But these are proving inadequate, so I am put on an adrenaline infusion. Two bags of rapid-pressure saline are pumped through my IV. I'm confused as to why there is a blood pressure cuff on the bag of saline and why there's a nurse pumping the bag like a bellows, as an infusion of artificial hydration disappears into my body like an illusion. Normally this would take an hour, but now it takes minutes. A doctor swabs my arm with alcohol – Listerine blue – then pushes a needle into my wrist for an arterial line. I close my eyes and see the needle deep within the pulsating blood of the artery. I know arterial lines go deep and worry that my wrist is going to be skewered. I brace myself for a dull thud against bone, but it never comes.

There's a herd of people in resus, and a doctor with a very loud voice is saying to me, 'We're looking for a secondary infection because of what's happening. This is very unusual.'

'Unusual' is not a word you want to hear when you're horizontal in a resus bay.

'But I haven't been sick,' I say over and over like an automaton, as though I am apologising.

Dad walks into the room in full PPE, his eyes watery and red-rimmed, his forehead flushed. I say 'I'll be fine' in a voice that doesn't quite feel like my own, and I say it because this is what he needs to hear. Family members aren't supposed to be in resus, and he has to leave. He plants a masked kiss on my forehead, and we say our customary 'I love you' to each other. I worry that he is worried.

Once I am stabilised, I'm taken to intensive care where the cadence is more subdued. The pace, the noise, the lights. It's like being transported from an EDM concert to a symphony orchestra. It's a friendlier place. More orderly. Nurses with soothing voices. Not long after I arrive, I need to pee, so two nurses put a plastic pan underneath me, but I know that it matters not how full my bladder gets, I will never be able to pee lying down. I've never been able to pee lying down. I bamboozle them into thinking I can walk to the bathroom in my hypotensive state. I have to concentrate to pretend I'm feeling fine and steady on my feet, and they help me shuffle to the enormous bathroom with my IV pole. They leave me on the toilet and then – out it rushes like a geyser. I am not a noisy pee-er. My pee has always sounded like a gentle trickle against porcelain, and while this pee isn't unusually loud, there is so much of it that the power behind it is leviathan. I sit on the toilet for several minutes waiting for my bladder to empty and I feel alive again. I shuffle back to bed with the nurses' help.

That evening, a sweet, burly doctor with a head full of chestnut curls attempts to insert a PICC line into my arm. He ultimately fails and is deeply apologetic. I had forewarned him that my left side was impenetrable after a deep vein thrombosis wrapped tentacles of clot around my basilic vein many years before. I pull my gown away so he can see the veins splayed across my chest like winding tributaries – blue streaks shooting up my neck and into my jaw, the blue fading as it hits the flush of my lower cheek. I am too exhausted for this to be a teaching moment. I am too sick to be combative, if being combative was something I did, which it's generally not. I soon find another doctor standing at the foot of my bed. My hands and arms are festooned with cannulas, the last of which has blown.

'We need to get a central line in, fast.'

In a whisper, I tell him that I am traumatised from having dozens of lines shoved into my neck, so he suggests a central line in my groin.

'Anywhere but my neck. Please,' I beg.

There are moments of dissociation, but then I feel the scalpel score my skin and the line being pushed into my femoral artery, the pain diffusing up and into my sacrum. I imagine that this is what it feels like to be stabbed.

*

For three days, antivirals and hydrocortisone are pushed through my CV line. The steroids make me feel ten feet tall and bulletproof and I talk and talk and talk. I send a photo of the line with its quad lumens lying across my mons pubis to my mum and sister, writing, 'I think I have herpes'. They both send back laughing emojis.

Afterwards, I find out that I am the only lung transplant recipient who has gone into septic shock from Covid; then months later I'm told it was total adrenal collapse. I keep being told I am lucky. I know that I'm lucky. Had I arrived at the hospital any later, I probably would have left the emergency department in a body bag.

On my last morning in the thoracic ward, a nurse removes my CV line. I watch the catheter slide out and notice how much longer and thicker it is in my groin than for any line I've had in my neck or chest. The blue tubing keeps coming, and for a moment, it feels like the nurse might have to walk backwards out of the room just to free it from my body. Holding pressure on the hole in my groin, I rest for a few minutes, then get up to brush my teeth. Leaning into the sink, I feel a creeping wetness. Lifting the bottom of my shorts, I see blood – beautiful, richly coloured arterial, impossibly red – coursing from my body. I'm fleetingly transfixed by the volume of blood dripping onto the linoleum, and it looks like the Red Cross emblem has melted onto my white underwear. I realise if I don't move, I'm going to exsanguinate, so I buzz for a nurse and walk back to bed. When she arrives, she stops short, eyes fixed on the blood streaking the floor.

'Oh no,' she says, running out of the room.

She returns with thick pads of gauze, bulky like menstrual pads, and presses them firmly into the valley between my pubic bone and upper thigh, as if delivering one long, unyielding CPR compression. Her palm remains anchored there even as my dad arrives to take me home. We wait twenty minutes. Then, cautiously, I pull on a fresh pair of knickers and go for a short walk. The wound has clotted. I toss my bloodstained underwear unceremoniously into the bin.

On the drive home, Dad and I sit side by side, our N95 masks giving us the look of solemn-faced ducks. I begin to cry. It feels like we're moving too fast.

'Dad, can you slow down?'

'I'm doing the speed limit, love.'

He drops me at home, then brings Billie back to me. She was all I could think about when I was in resus – her, and how I'd promised my publisher I wouldn't expire before my memoir's launch date.

Billie belts through the door, her paws scrambling to gain purchase on the wooden floorboards. She finds enough traction to jump all over me, but I am feeling fragile, and as it turns out, so is she. I walk over to my carpetbag, pick it up and urge myself to push through the weight – not just the weight of the bag, but of the moment. I put it away, so she knows I am staying.

Judith Huang

Ivan and Turtle

I.

Ivan the giant knew the way out of this place.

His legs are long enough that sitting out here, in this little pavilion out the back where we can sometimes exercise and mostly smoke, he could easily scale that wall. He could easily scale that bright yellow wall and be out in a jiffy.

He's a tough old geezer who has done almost everything imaginable in his long life. The only reason he's in here is cos he figures he's safer than out there, and he knows his Sheila, the love of his life, is still thinking of him because he can see the videos she uploads to YouTube, old ones from the 90s and brand-new ones of their beautiful daughters.

In this one, she's a blonde bombshell with pitch-black smoky eyes like two bullet holes from which stars stare out, crawling all over the long mahogany dining table, pointing her perfect boobs and ass towards a young man with a lock of jet-black hair falling over his face and an expression of studied nonchalance: young Ivan, maybe twenty years ago, maybe thirty.

'You were very good-looking,' I say as the blonde topples all the cutlery and smashes the wineglasses. She crawls and lies on her back spilling red wine over her cleavage, glaring at the camera.

Ivan the giant, old and grizzled and sixty-something, is not good-looking. His mismatched eyes look far into the distance over his broken nose, broken in so many places it looks like a well-worn rock. He has a series of scars running around his neck which make it look like he's been stapled together.

When he told me about what they'd done to him, what they'd

made him sacrifice for Sheila, he shows me another huge ugly scar running all the way up his left shin 'when they amputated me and put this new cyborg leg into me'. But no matter what, he still moves like a rock star. It helps that he's so huge. He must be at least seven feet. I am a tiny Asian hobbit next to him.

Ivan the giant likes me best of all the people in here because I believe every word he says.

I like him for the same reason. There is not one black hole in the heart of humanity that we won't believe possible, and why not? They've already done everything imaginable to us.

Ivan the giant makes me feel like Sophie in *The BFG*, and we believe each other. How else would they have put us in here together except to see if we recognise each other after all those other lifetimes? I tell him I read about him in a book when I was a child, a book about a giant and an orphan and the Queen of England, and he nods. Ivan already knows.

Ivan the giant, when he isn't helping me put Australia back together again, spends a lot of time staring at the tiny blaring screen of his smartphone. He watches out for messages from his Sheila and his daughters, who are also blonde-haired, gorgeous bombshells.

Here's one of them in a sky-blue convertible so her yellow hair waves like a brilliant flame in the golden hour, wearing a cowboy hat and driving a straight road down into the world. 'That's her way of giving me the finger,' says Ivan. 'That was my car, see, and she's made this video so I'll know she's taken it. I know she's mad at me, but that's how we are.'

Ivan has nobody on this side of the country because of them. 'Implants,' he says. 'The implants in my neck transmit everything to them. For a mission.' He bends down to make me touch the ridges. I feel like I'm touching the neck of an ancient tiger. There's definitely something other than bone buried beneath.

I believe him because they wouldn't stop at anything to create a perfect soldier. They would spare no expense, would bury any scruple.

I knew this because they did this to me too, and they were a lot less subtle in my country. When my green silk blouse tears I tell Ivan they cut off my left breast and then reattached a new one while I slept. I'm an Amazon, a disposable warrior, a child soldier designed to fight their wars. He nods.

Ivan was a child soldier too. They made them super-strong and super-intelligent, able to withstand searing, crushing pain. One time, they made him sacrifice a limb to save his Sheila.

'That's why they can never separate us,' says Ivan. 'I gave my life for hers, and she gave her life for mine, we love each other and always will. It's a bond they'll never break. It doesn't matter if we don't talk for years, we understand each other. We'll always be together in here.' He taps his giant heart.

'Many times, in many worlds. Sometimes she wore a different face – you know, virtual reality, but it's just a skin. Sometimes they put us in different bodies, but me and my Sheila, we always recognised each other – but it was our souls – our souls always knew.'

II.

Ivan and I are in the dining room, and I am concerned with fixing the country back together again.

Fixing the country. That's the important thing. Now I know they have violated the vulnerable, taken children like Ivan before he grew into a giant, recruited for their stupid, secret, sadistic, unnecessary wars; now that we know they have raped, mind and soul and body, making them fight psychonautic, psychosomatic, intergalactic wars; now that we know they have genocided the blameless, colonised lands and destroyed them; now they have hidden the country itself in the dining room and waged war on the soul of the continent, we must fix the country back together again.

The puzzle pieces lie in front of me, and I organise them to put poor Australia fair together again. This impossible puzzle, the one inmates never attempt, because who wants to put together a puzzle of Australia when there is food to be eaten, nice, creamy, fatty food, and pills and pills and pills, and reality TV, just as creamy and fatty and bad for you?

'We must be in the most boring iteration of *Big Brother*,' says John, beautiful, angelic John, John of the clear blue eyes, well-spoken John in his incongruous streetwear. John-too-good-to-be-true.

After John arrived, he and I played chess in the dining room night after night after the sun set. We started playing in autumn, and then continued to play even as the bedrooms grew infernally cold. I knew they kept bodies back in section C because the air was always coldest there. And there was that door, with the metal fastenings and reinforced hinges, that was always locked. Maybe they brought John out through there. The John who taught me chess was the good John. Then John turned. It wasn't fair, what they did to John. It's not fair, what they do to us.

III.

It was around this time I feared for my life and I tried to plead for it through the beauty of my music. How unfair that the most sublime, the most piteous of my improvisations flared through the wooden upright piano here, where the wise are locked up, where the blameless are put away. Outside, the silent and undeclared war rages, and in here are the only people who dare cry the truth, in songs that declare:

This generation imprisons its prophets in madhouses and makes madmen kings.

Ivan and I are playing magic on the keys, I on bass and he on treble, and all the other inmates are cheering. They know that this is really something, something that spits in the face of this mad world and our jailers.

It is not arpeggios and it is not melodies, it is not sad and it is not happy, it moves from key to key like a lean, bright wolf exploring new terrain. Ivan's love for Sheila and my mourning for John, who has been missing at least two weeks. So the song is sad and blissful and romantic and yearning and slow, and then it is hopeful and gorgeous and tin-tin-tinnitus as we hit the keys and pluck the strings. Whatever it is, it is not mad.

Time is weird in here. But with our music we are dividing time in the way it ought to be, through song. Ivan picks up the guitar that is missing the E string but sounds amazing anyway and I sing along while playing, which I could not do outside. Maybe this place is magic.

What we want is not absolution. What we want is innocence.

IV.

Ivan has been everywhere so of course Ivan has been to Vietnam. I have been nowhere near Vietnam but Ivan has been around a lot longer than I have, so maybe it was another round. How many times have I incarnated on this plane? Nobody ever knows.

'I dreamt I was a turtle, trying to swim away from people who wanted me dead,' I told Ivan while we smoked in the pavilion. 'They made me into a turtle and they wanted you to hunt me to prove your loyalty. You hid me in a wheelbarrow and wheeled me to the ocean.'

'I know.' Ivan had tears in his eyes. He dragged on his cigarette and then let a puff of cloud out of his gnarly old mouth. We were facing the car park beyond the yellow wall, which only contained white cars. Sedans, SUVs, hatchbacks, trucks, every single one of them Stormtrooper white, like Darth Vader's secret multistorey civil service. Every morning I watched the cars come in, in a long white row; every evening most of them left. The ones left behind were like so many white stones in the collection of a sky god even bigger, stronger, and more gnarly than Ivan.

'Back in 'Nam,' growled Ivan. 'They wanted us to shoot kids. I couldn't, I refused. There was this one, this young one who I knew wouldn't stand a chance. But she'd been so sweet, bringing me food when they starved us. I called her Turtle.'

'You were just doing your job,' I said, watching the tears as big as buckets form and roll down Ivan's cheeks. 'I know you tried.'

'I put you – I put you in my pocket,' Ivan said, miming it. 'I said, keep quiet, while the others aren't looking.'

'I did. I did.' I was crying. I don't know what pills they had given me that day but it didn't matter, it was all true, all of it.

'I made it, Ivan,' I said. His fingers were trembling as the ash from his cigarette peppered the air.

'I never knew if that kid lived or died, all I knew was I was ordered to shoot the moment any of you ran.'

'It's okay, Ivan,' I said. Didn't I write all those stories about turtles? How could it not have been me in another life? Ivan the giant has lived in samsara for four times the lifespan of me, one little turtle, and he has his hands stained with blood, for loving his country, for loving his Sheila; that's how they manipulated him into shooting little starved Asian kids in the back, running away from the men who caught and sold them and here we were, Ivan and I, holding each other in this pavilion at the end of the earth absolving murder, life, death and this thing they call madness.

'Turtle ...' Ivan's cigarette falls to the ground among the hundreds of stubs that defy the 'no smoking allowed on hospital premises' sign. We embrace, crying each other's tears. He believes everything – that I was brought up in a child harem for my country's royal family, trained in the arts of statecraft and propaganda before being exiled for choosing a commoner over a prince; that I have been traded hand under fist by my own relatives for power, wealth, influence; that even now there were secret agencies watching me – not that they weren't watching everyone.

I weep, and clutch Ivan's middle, my tears soaking into his t-shirt while he cradles me in the pavilion that smells of smoke.

V.

When they took Ivan away, he was wearing red pyjamas – shocking deep crimson instead of his rock-and-roll black t-shirt and jeans.

He didn't look so good. Had they reprogrammed him? He sat in the dining room to watch YouTube again. After the third video of a different gorgeous blonde who was definitely his Sheila, I asked, 'When's the last time you actually video-chatted her?'

Ivan bristled. 'She's busy but we don't need to call to know how each other feel.'

'You know these days it could just be an AI feeding you new content, it could be a bot you're chatting to on text.'

'She can take care of herself.'

'You say she's working – is she working for them?'

'She's a capable woman, she does a lot of work for them.'

'Ivan, she needs you. You need to get off your ass, get out of here, and go find her.'

'I said she's working.'

'Probably on her back!' And the expression that flits over Ivan's face means he knows it's true. A woman as beautiful as that, there was no way they weren't making her turn tricks.

'Sheila can take care of herself.'

'She needs you, Ivan.'

Ivan keeps quiet.

'What happened to the guy who fought in every secret war? What happened to you? Remember you defeated the other side in the bowels of the earth?'

But Ivan is sullen. He plays the next video, the renegades running away, true love driving them on. The boy is played by Asa Butterfield, his eyes blue and far apart, his face childish, innocent.

'They reskinned it,' says Ivan, softly.

'What do you mean? That's Asa Butterfield.'

'They just Photoshop another face on, but I did that, that was me.'

I watch the video with him. The police close in on the couple. The girl a gold blur of blonde hair, Asa's eyes wide and round.

'It's all the same war. They put us through these simulations, tell us it's a different one, that we need to save the world. Look – the soundtrack – it's exactly the same. The same fucking song and they think we don't notice.'

Ivan is more excited about the generic score than about the love of his life being fucked over.

'But what about Sheila? Sheila is real. Your Sheila. She needs you.'

'Sheila can look after herself.'

'You're a fool,' I say, crying. 'So fucking smart but you're a fool. How can you sit there, knowing …'

Ivan closes his eyes. His fingers touch his collarbone, fingering the metal staples under the skin.

'They can already hear you. With this implant they can hear everything. It's no use.'

Overwhelming sadness floods me. He's given up. He pretends to be a rebel, but they broke him. This is what our heroes look like four decades later, old giants with stapled-up chests and black exhaustion behind their eyes. Old giants felled, wearing dark red hospital pyjamas.

'It's too late. You can't split one over zero,' he says.

'Oh yes you can.'

'No, you can't. You get infinity.'

'What do you get when you divide ten by three?'

'It goes on forever.'

'So? Doesn't that mean anything to you?'

'How about a hundred? What do you get when you divide a hundred by three?'

'Ah, that's the question!' Ivan perks up.

'What if I am the 33rd degree?'

I flip a piece of the empty ocean onto the incomplete puzzle and it lands face-up, exactly where it was missing. Exactly.

'What's the chance of that?'

'What if we have infinite lives and an infinity to live them in?'

'Come on, Turtle. I'm tired.'

'You're not tired,' I say, three years old at heart and pulling on my grandfather's toe.

'You're Ivan. Now go get her, tiger.'

That was the last time I saw Ivan.

VI.

Months later, groggy and discharged, I will not even extend to myself the same kindness of so much belief, so much trust, so much love, as I extended to Ivan.

I fucked John in my dreams for days after Ivan left: blonde, handsome, young, well-spoken John with the eyelashes to die for. After sunset we played chess. Every night, chess and conversation, and a shared cigarette out in the pavilion, fucking each other with our eyes, until the day he leaned against the yellow wall and sneered, 'Ivan must have been pretty damn busy playing in every rock band from about 1970 to 1992, eh?', and then somehow the spell was broken. But I cannot blame John for hanging on to too much sanity; after all he had poisoned me twice and who knew who he was really working for?

But even with Ivan gone, and even with John whispering in my ear, I still remember Ivan lifting me onto the bench in the pavilion to show me just how easy it would be to get out of here.

Ivan the giant could stride over the walls, easy, and yet he chose to be in here with me.

I fucked John in my dreams nightly until the fucker betrayed me. I haven't seen either of them since and I probably never will. In places like this, there's no returning; all the people would be different.

The day he betrayed me, in that awful pastel dining room with the taunting windows, John told me he'd done a Judas, told the nurses to discharge me and this was our last supper, I said, 'The point of this place isn't to impress you, the point of this place is to get out.' And that was when he knew he'd done the right thing.

That was John for you; at least he had the courtesy to tell me that the day Ivan and I played the duet on the piano was the day he yearned to play.

Ivan and I both knew the way out of this place. He'd lifted me casually with one arm as though I had weighed nothing, so I, too, could see the easy way out. But why would we? This place, this place where we met and stood together, this place was sacred ground.

The multitude of things that we lived through, in the time we stood there, was extraordinary and world-encompassing. In those nameless, uncounted days, we lived a hundred times more than a human should. For a moment, we became the load-bearing Atlases of the world. There we were, shouldering its weight, but the madness blessed it, and perhaps because we were mad, it was borne, and the world continued.

So what if it wasn't a bare fact that we experienced it? We bore it as though we had, fully believed it, fully suffered it. In that sacred, holy place where the cigarette butts made the air ashen, we were the only real beings, and there, like Man and God, we forgave each other.

What we wanted was innocence. What we received was absolution.

VII.

Ivan the giant was always my hero. Because every kids' movie, no matter how flim-flam and fake, was real to the children who watched them and in every one of them Ivan, Ivan the giant, Ivan the Aussie alcoholic, Ivan the washed-up rock star, Ivan the psych ward patient, he had saved us all. Every time we sat down before a screen, console in hand, we re-enacted Ivan's run, Ivan's story, the life of Ivan, saviour of mankind, and the extraordinary thing is that the story was true. Is true. Is always true.

And here I had met the real Ivan. How can I not look up at his craggy neck, the painful metal staples protruding from scarred flesh, and say I was not his Turtle?

It was Ivan's last gift to me, completing those bits of pure blue ocean, as blue as John's eyes.

Weeks later, I was discharged and out in the world again, that fake world, sleeping nearly eighteen hours a day. But for one glorious day, the day when Ivan left, the puzzle lay enshrined, complete, on the dining room table. When I saw it, I smiled, then I laughed when I saw the note in Ivan's scrawl, stuck under the bottom right corner of the continent.

The bastards put in extra pieces! The game's rigged, Turtle. Take care.

Sure enough, there were seven whole extra pieces of empty ocean that didn't fit anywhere.

I admired the country we'd fixed together for a minute, then swept the whole thing back into the box. I threw away the extra ocean pieces so the next hero would have a better chance.

What a war, what a war.

What a game.

Ariel Riveros

Hache

Away from the regard
of the Everyone

I see an idea through a window.
I become its faceted clarity briefly.

It steps softly. I ravel back through lenses to walk among
Italian technicians

discussing German research on double French. This fugue
splashing through

song and semaphore saw melees in galleys, cloud reading,
passage of tortoises,

eclipsed retinas, twisted tongues
and parlance of botany

breathing with plants. I was told to expect austerity in the
market of stompers.

Senserrate

These fingerprints tell
stories of sands
spouting to shade

of inherited identity thefts.
Tracts of prints loyal
to love and dreams

of tenseless limbs.
No arch struggle,
no voice from the street

to bust me mid-grift.
We're laid out so
languorous that our

presence is sensed
in neighbouring precincts
and we run into ourselves

on our way to the business district
scrimmaging for a bar entrance
to drink cold and quiet among

carpets, turning to night.
You send me every heart emoji
to feast on like a wolf

Of wolves bringing the trail
back to loop like planets in
the knitting that returns

rarely in lifetimes, singularly
when we repeat our tracks,
where we can boast we leapt

the whole way on the ensuing
cycles even though our footsteps
push deeper, push back to

our heeling as orbits of
natural numbers replay when in skies

Chronesthesia III

Before we leave
I've left the tracked traffic
to resting,

Emerge a cloaked signal from
barrelling worlds.

I hear out. Ships' sprayed noise
like spume buildings, seabed
washing.

Before we go clank on
the scaffolding, I am practising
extensing, cube by cube like a toy.

Play quartet, have habits, find
passage with these colours and
remember the date you re-enact.

A photo of infrared makes pink and
the night felt untreated. So it goes
to the last occurrence of it.

The association is the rose gold sky and bridge walking past
midnight in a straight line.

You leapt with all the build and guile
between two times at once

Encamp

When I speak to your bones
I want nothing but the circulation
of peace – tender junctures.

Skin is wound around
The moon in brightest bloom
Running like the lives of saints.

I hum my words
Like deep swum fish
And a tone

From Herculaneum's spectres
Playing through
Your skeleton.

Here I sit like ore
In the stone,
A hundredweight pace.

You sit with me at night
And light a lamp to
Wait for the wet world.

Akii Ngo

Why?/Reason

> There is no greater agony than bearing an untold story inside you
>
> – Maya Angelou

Growing up, I've always tried to reassure myself that everything traumatic and deeply unpleasant that I've had to go through (and continue to go through) is for a reason. And one of the main reasons is to help others, create positive change and to share my story in hopes that it inspires (not in an inspirational porn way!) and/or provides much-needed comfort, hope and kinship to those suffering, especially in times of endless despair and hopelessness.

Life for me hasn't been the easiest. It's actually been pretty darned fked up and really rough.

You see, I was born with Necrotising Enterocolitis – a life-threatening, rare condition with a 50 per cent mortality rate. Within the first couple hours of my birth, I took my first flight. (And considering the fact that I'm an avid traveller now, I joke that I definitely started real early!) An emergency chopper took my fragile, prematurely dying body from Geraldton Regional Hospital to Perth's Princess Margaret Hospital for life-saving surgery where portions of my gangrenous bowels were removed. I was incubated for a majority of my first year of life, until they grew, could be repaired and sewn back together.

Not the best start, huh? But what made matters so much more challenging is that my parents were refugees who fled the Vietnam War, arriving after living for years in squalid conditions in a Thai refugee camp. They arrived in the coast of Western Australia and settled in a small town, eight hours away from Perth, called Geraldton. It was very common for refugees to be sent to very regional or rural areas (most of which were extremely not diverse and full of racism). My parents met, married and gave birth to my older brother after years of living in the Thai refugee camps as they fled war-torn Vietnam. When they made the treacherous voyage to Australia, they had an infant in tow (my brother) and my maternal parent was pregnant with my sister. Can you imagine what they went through to make it safely (at least physically) to Australia? The suffering and trauma they must've witnessed and experienced trying to find safe passage to a faraway land with no guarantees, no family, no friends, no kinship, no language and no familiar culture.

As an adult, I can acknowledge and appreciate the challenges, difficulties and inconceivable amount of trauma my parents lived through. It explains why my childhood wasn't the best (massive understatement!). I'd like to think that I know truly within my heart that they just did what they could with what they had and what they knew at the time, in addition to their own severe unresolved trauma and pain. And, despite being estranged, I guess that's all I could have ever asked of them. But as a child I didn't recognise that I was parenting my parents while I experienced constant pain and hurt – mentally, emotionally, spiritually and physically – as a result of my ongoing complex chronic conditions alongside the multitude of cross-cultural clashes, beliefs, attitudes and the confusion of growing up in 90s Australia with strict Asian refugee migrant parents.

My eyes immediately well with tears as I think back to my childhood and how much I hurt. If I could communicate to my younger teary-eyed and very suicidal selves, I would tell them to cry as much as they need to but reassure them that *it's okay* and *things will and do get better*. Eventually, I got a tattoo with the words 'this too, shall pass' to remind myself of everything I've survived, against all the odds.

My complex chronic conditions and various disabilities meant that I had to become very independent, very quickly. My parents could not speak English (their education level back in Vietnam was below Grade 4) and no matter how many interpreters were booked, it was *never* the right dialect – this meant I had to interpret and translate for my parents during my own medical appointments. Frustrations grew increasingly around my lack of ability to interpret (I have no formal Vietnamese language education) and their lack of ability to understand. Eventually, having them around 'cost' (mentally, emotionally and capacity-wise) more than it was worth. (Imagine being told you've got a tumour in your chest that needs to be removed ASAP and your parents getting angry at you for not interpreting fast enough?!) So, from about age ten or eleven, I began travelling (via many buses and trains) to attend all my appointments alone.

'Life wouldn't be so hard if it wasn't for you,' my maternal parent would regularly exclaim when she was frustrated or upset with me. My disabilities and never-ending health issues didn't make things easier on the family, especially to parents who fled to the other side of the world for a better life. I was constantly the topic of conversation or blame for things going wrong. My older siblings stayed out of it, and essentially away from me. Growing up, I never felt like I had anyone in my corner, ever, even during some of my most difficult times – surgeries, hospitalisations, bullying at school, depression, anxiety, severe self-harm, suicide attempts, psychiatric holds, homelessness, family violence, abusive intimate relationships and severe identity crises.

Studying hard, getting the best grades and being a high achiever from a young age were culturally required of me. Ask any first-generation immigrant Asian child out there and I am certain that 99 per cent of them would agree. We were regularly reminded of all they (our parents) went through to create a better life for us in Australia and if we didn't work hard according to them (demonstrated by academic excellence), we weren't valuing their sacrifice. Not to mention the hard work they were doing in Australia as farm labourers to ensure we were fed and clothed. In other words, if there is a roof over your head and food on your table, you have nothing to complain or be sad about. If you did, you were ungrateful! Expectations were always very high: we had to meet a certain standard, and the need to brag within our social culture was unrelenting – 'saving face' amongst peers and community was crucial. And despite my progressively worsening health and the fact that I spent a majority of Year 12 *living* (and yes, I do mean living, as I was an inpatient for over four months) at the Adelaide Children's Hospital, I still managed to achieve an above 90 ATAR and get into my first preference (Nutrition and Dietetics). It wasn't medicine (which, of course, my parents wanted) but it was close 'enough'. I went to university, graduated and got a 'proper job' even before I graduated, and eventually managed to complete four more tertiary qualifications. So, even after it all, I still did everything they wanted me to do and more, even though I left home at sixteen, pushing hard in order to stay alive, especially when my mental health and self-harm was at its worst.

On top of the strict rules and high standards, I was never permitted to do 'Australian' or average 'White people' things like ride a bike to school, attend school functions, hang out with friends in the neighbourhood or even attend school camps. Each year, a student from each grade was selected to win an all-expenses-paid week away called the 'Success Trip' and although I won it three years in a row, I was never permitted to go. I will never know what it is like to go on a school trip. I was never allowed to dye my hair or have piercings – originality and uniqueness were frowned upon. We were consistently reminded to 'put our heads down, work hard, don't make trouble and "blend in" – avoid drawing any attention to yourself'.

Our family wasn't close. We never really talked, never ever said 'I love you' or shared our feelings – a very common trait of Asian households as feelings are considered 'weak'. Vietnamese, Chinese, Japanese, and Cambodian customs and traditions are very hierarchical and patriarchal in nature, with clear familial roles and responsibilities. My brother's job was to tell me and my sister what to do regarding chores, cooking and cleaning. And children are always required and expected to help parents and cultural elders when asked (more like told) – I 'lucked' out in this area in a way as my brother and sister were expected to help on the farm after school and on weekends. However, I was exempt from it most of the time due to my disabilities and health challenges. My 'job/responsibility' was therefore, to be the homemaker – from around age ten, I could confidently cook a meal from scratch and ensured I had food on the table for when my parents arrived home from work. This was very different to all my non-Asian friends and often made me feel sad, upset, lonely and that I was missing out.

Beauty standards were also very different. In Australia, having tanned, sun-kissed skin, thinness (with curves in all the right places) and full lips (back in the 90s) was envied whereas Asian culture was the opposite, with white skin, big eyes, being Asian thin and petite, and having small lips were the epitome of beauty. These beauty standards directly impacted me and my self-esteem as I was *constantly* told I was too chubby, my lips were too ugly and I definitely was not pretty enough *especially* because of my monolid eyes (aka 'small squinty Asian eyes') and my numerous surgical scars (as a result of my various lifesaving infant and childhood surgeries). When I was eleven or twelve years old, my birth-giver brought me to Vietnam and forced me to get double eyelid surgery. I was kicking and screaming as the surgeon had sliced through one of my eyelids when my dad came running in and said, 'Enough!! Can't you tell that our child does not want this?!' as he picked me up and took me right out of there. I sobbed for days and still, to this day, almost twenty years later, have a little scar on my right eyelid to remind me I was never good enough for her. Comments about my surgical scars and never being able to wear a bikini, etc., were constant – but also, I'd have to lose weight and be 'skinny' enough to wear one anyway.

In seeking affection, comfort and what I thought was 'love' at such a formative time in my life, I entered relationships at a young age and became a serial monogamist – obviously, upon reflection, it was clear I was yearning for stability and comfort – something I was desperately missing at home and in life. My first relationship was at age twelve, with someone four years my senior. I had a crush on this person as he was a friend of my sister and I only wanted to please and impress him – thinking to myself how lucky I was to have someone like him be interested in me. In the name of 'love', I let him pressure and talk me into things a fourteen-year-old should never have done in the name of him not wanting to be an eighteen-year-old virgin. We dated for four years and when we broke up for good, he relentlessly stalked me, threatened me and terrified me. A police report (which my biology teacher encouraged and accompanied me to make) was the only thing that deterred him when it got too much. The next relationship was more or less the same, except for physical violence which resulted in my spinal injury – with daily pain and consequences I still deal with to this day. I continued to date men who hurt me and made me feel less than. 'Partners' who belittled me, made me believe in love and then broke me, betrayed me and hurt me in more ways than I can bear to describe. I eventually realised I was simply accepting the love I thought I deserved (and which was modelled to me) – which wasn't much at all. As a result of all this, along with ableism and plain ol' homo and transphobia, I never dared to explore the concept of disability pride, my (VERY) Queer sexuality and gender identities until much later in life.

I moved out of home when I finished high school and started university. I was barely sixteen and lived with random housemates Ifound online. It was a tough transition but because I had been taking care of myself since I was so young, I was fairly confident that I would be okay. My mental health improved drastically and while I dealt with many, many more years of unsavoury and sometimes very unsafe relationships, the stress on my mental health and well-being from my family life was much less of an issue. Over time, my relationship with my father improved and we occasionally keep in touch. And while it pains me, I am completely estranged from my siblings and birth-giver (so Mother's Day, Father's Day, Christmas and so on are not easy times of the year). But I know it's for the best. I need to protect my peace and choose myself, no matter how hard it is to do.

Growing up in Australia came with its challenges but it also came with so many wonderful opportunities. Firstly, it gave me life. Without being born in a country of universal healthcare, I am certain I would not have survived. Secondly, it gave me education and opportunity. Once I finished my university degree and had some experience under my belt, I very spontaneously did something I never thought I would or could ever do. I moved alone to a foreign country (Japan), where I knew no-one and didn't know the language. Living abroad for eighteen months completely alone at nineteen years old was one of the most exhilarating experiences I've had – it was the first time in my entire life, I did something for myself and only myself. I learned so much about who I was, how resilient and brave I truly am and can be. However, unfortunately due to the degenerative nature of my disabilities, I physically and logistically could never do that now, which just makes me even gladder I did it. Though, admittedly at times, I do feel some grief for the Akii that could. Regardless – I am so thankful for that experience and leap of faith because for the first time in my life, I truly put myself first and did something just for me. This enabled me to learn self-discovery, the power and bravery of being okay with being entirely alone, inner strength, self-advocacy, resilience and self-respect. It embedded in me an immense sense of adventure and wanderlust. As a child I used to be terrified of change of any kind, dreading it constantly, but now I've learned to embrace it wholeheartedly.

I have now been living on my own with no family or familial support for almost seventeen years. I have been (not always successfully) navigating my relentless complex chronic illnesses, severely debilitating chronic pain, multiple neurodivergencies (Autistic, ADHD, complex-PTSD) and numerous disabilities, essentially all on my own. And not in spite of, but because of them, I have subsequently built my life dedicated to making positive change and helping others from a big-picture, systemic, population-level perspective (via campaigns, policies, reforms and such) using my widespread professional expertise and extensive diverse, intersectional lived and living experiences. On a micro level, I am often the unofficial mentor to all my friends (especially my disabled ones) – being the behind-the-scenes cheerleader for all, always a sounding board and advice-giver when asked or needed.

Additionally, I am an internationally published model and have been professionally modelling (with a touch of acting and voiceover work) for over six years, working with small and large brands – I've been on storefronts, buses, billboards, buildings, magazines, banks and runways across Australia. I do it because of the critical need for greater representation.

I am being the change I wanted, never witnessed and most importantly, *needed*, growing up. Representation matters – so I am doing my part to ensure diverse, intersectional beings are considered, valued and uplifted within spaces we usually are not: fashion and beauty.

All of the work I do and who I ultimately am links back to the very beginning of this piece; my reason for trying to make sense of everything. Through the constant suffering, pain and endless life challenges, I searched for a sense of purpose: to use my various experiences and stories to create genuine sustainable change and make positive differences. My advocacy takes various forms including but not limited to providing extensive lived experience advice and advocacy in all levels of government and working within university-facilitated research projects focusing on marginalised communities. I provide training and consultancy (in accessibility, disability justice, neurodivergence, LGBTQIA+, anti-racism, violence prevention and intersectionality and all aspects of diversity and inclusion) to build the capacity of organisations, companies and business of all sizes. I am also a passionate lived experience and intersectional keynote presenter, facilitator and host/MC who has the honour and privilege of being part of countless events of all kinds.

It's ultimately about pushing for genuine non-tokenistic intersectional and diverse representation. Being the representation I needed but never experienced growing up.

Fighting what often feels like an excruciating uphill battle so that ultimately no-one suffers, especially alone, anymore. I don't really know how many people I've helped, motivated or changed for the better, but if I have made one person feel less alone, not 'broken', ashamed, scared, or embarrassed, but cared for, loved, proud, unapologetically themselves or less afraid, then that's all that truly matters. A lot of what I do is not just a 'job' but is fundamentally part of the very fabric of my existence. And I am so incredibly grateful and privileged to do it each and every day, even on days where the barriers that exist for someone like me feel beyond impossible.

Arty Owens

Just relax

I'm confronted by beige tiles. A drain in the centre of the room. A damp floor. The sensory deprivation pod looks like a sleek white tic tac.

I ready myself to enter, trying not to think about whether somebody has pissed in it. Luxury with all the discomforts of a public pool.

My friend is in the room next door. This stuff usually isn't for me but she swears by it. 'It really helps you get perspective.' She does it every year and really wanted to share the experience with me.

For love and perspective I open the hatch and descend.

The salty water pricks my skin. Seeps into my ears. I was worried I might feel closed in, but I stare into endless dark. I guess it's more like floating in an abyss.

I don't like this.

But I haven't really given it a go. I need to be more open to the experience. I'm so buoyant, I feel like I'm fighting the water. Don't fight the water. Be open. C'mon. Be open.

In the dark I start to feel myself dissolve, untethering from a physical realm, reabsorbed into the wider fabric of the universe. It is exactly what my friend described. I'm not feeling that enlightened sense of perspective I'm sure she is experiencing in the room next door.

My slippery hands reach for the walls. Looking for a ridge, for a way to hold tight. What if I let go and can't find them again?

My nipples are freezing nails. My skin an itchy fire. I am really fighting the saline now, trying to reach the bottom. I'm a writhing worm in the Dead Sea, desperate to reach the shore. I think I've created a current. Choppy sea waters are making my hands slip on the pod walls.

I am Jack, scrambling to get on the door with Rose.

Maybe I'm not giving this a proper go? Maybe I'm doing it wrong? I should at least see this to the end? I try to control my breathing. Do some meditation shit. But every time I let go I scramble to anchor myself. I must be tethered to this earth. I have to hold myself together. I close my eyes and wait for this experience to be over.

A lifetime later soft meditation music lets me know I can leave and I launch myself out like a newborn giraffe. Slick. Frightened. Shaking in a beige room with an extremely internal scream.

'How was it?' asks the receptionist.

'Great,' I say, glancing sideways at my friend's peaceful expression. Unbothered by the thick smell of incense and painfully repetitive relaxation music. The glow of new-found insight like a halo around her. To be fair, I think I've gotten some new insight about myself too. I don't think I have the same glow as her though.

'My skin was a little irritated—'

'That's normal.' The receptionist cuts me off with a wave of her hand. 'You need at least two more sessions to get used to it. Do you want to book now?'

'Thank you so much,' I say, backing away. 'I'll think about it.'

Ethan Patrick

Learning to live with being 'disabled'

From the moment I emerged into the world, I was fighting for my life.

Born eleven weeks premature and weighing just 1212 grams (2lbs 11oz.), my survival was never guaranteed and it took months of round-the-clock care, supplemental oxygen and no small amount of hope to keep me alive.

But it wasn't until about a week after my birth that my parents realised that if I survived, my journey, *our* journey, was far from over. An MRI had revealed that there was clear damage to my brain.

As is always the case with brain damage, the doctors told my parents that they couldn't predict how it would affect me. They prepared them for the worst, telling them I might never be able to walk, talk or even function independently. My parents had to confront the fact that they might be my carers for the rest of my life.

I was eventually diagnosed with Cerebral Palsy (CP), a condition that affects the signals between my brain and my muscles. While early diagnosis is incredibly important for early intervention, and is something that my family and I are forever thankful for, it also means that I have never known life without being referred to as 'disabled'.

This wasn't a choice I made, this label I was given, it just was. It was the first thing people would learn about me, often before they even knew my name, if they ever learned my name at all.

And for a very long time, I hated it.

But to be very clear, it wasn't my disability I hated, it was being *labelled* as disabled. Now, some of you might ask 'What's the difference?'

Well, as I said in the beginning, from the moment I emerged into the world, disability was an unshakeable, unquestionable part of my reality, even during that short time that we didn't know it yet. Some of my earliest memories are of hospitals, surgeries and treatments.

Suffice to say, I always knew that my body didn't work the same way as everyone else's, but for a long time, it was just part of my life. My family had never treated me any differently than my brother or my cousins, so I didn't understand why it mattered.

But when I started school, suddenly I was being told that there were so many things I *couldn't* do because I was disabled.

Like going down a slide. Running. Climbing the playground. Playing with my friends without someone watching my every move.

I didn't understand, because I *could* do those things. I did them differently than everyone else, sure, but I could do it.

Now, it's worth mentioning that despite how I might've made it sound, my disability doesn't necessarily make me stand out like I'm carrying a giant neon sign (even if that's how it feels sometimes). I can proudly announce that despite the doctors' warnings, I can walk, talk, drive and (mostly) function independently.

Other than the limp that gets more noticeable when I'm tired, the tripping over nothing and the equally terrible motor skills (my sincerest apologies to anyone who has been stuck behind me at the Myki barriers), my condition isn't always obvious at first glance.

In fact, I can confidently say at least 30 per cent of people will notice my perpetually untied shoelaces before my disability.

But this wasn't always the case.

As a child, my knees and feet were turned inwards and my right arm was often curled up by my ear, in a position affectionately known as my 'dinosaur arm'. Whatever subtlety I have now is a result of years of physical therapy, countless surgeries and no small amount of stubbornness.[1]

---

1 As a result of muscle tension, the 'dinosaur arm' still makes an appearance when I'm stressed. I usually don't notice until someone in front of me brakes quite suddenly and I nearly smack myself in the face.

Regardless of my physical differences, my cognitive function was – and still is – unaffected. But at my relatively small mainstream school, I was the only exposure most kids and even lots of the adults had ever had to disability in their day-to-day lives. As a result, despite my protests about the limitations being imposed on me – which were far stricter than those placed on my able-bodied peers – I was seen as incapable of deciding for myself, by adults who had a preconceived idea of what 'disability' meant.

Luckily, my parents not only allowed me the freedom to explore my abilities at home, but tirelessly advocated for my independence in school, something for which I'm forever grateful.

But my parents weren't there every day, so from an early age, becoming an educator and an advocate for not only myself, but others with disability, was not a choice, but just a way of life. So, it was often a case of being disabled first and an individual second.

And despite everyone's best efforts, the damage had already been done. Intentional or not, that was when I started to realise that according to the world around me, to be 'disabled' was a bad thing.

This label, which had previously been simply part of who I was, started to feel like a curse.

It was why strangers would call me a 'poor thing' or apologise to my parents. Why they talked about me like I wasn't there or like I was a baby.

In my mind, it seemed that to be disabled meant being automatically defined by everything I couldn't do. It meant there was something fundamentally wrong with the way I was. Something to be ashamed of.

I wanted to hide it somewhere where no-one would ever find it and never talk about it. But with my body suffering from the same lack of subtlety as the rest of me, that wasn't a luxury I was often afforded, especially as a child.

So why am I talking about it now, if I never wanted to before?

Because in some ways my previous statement isn't exactly accurate. I delight in regaling people with the weird and wonderful experiences I've had because of my disability, from the gory details of surgery to the sometimes-bewildering interactions with strangers.

Like the woman who offered to perform a healing ritual on me in the middle of a supermarket.

Or the man who spent ten minutes trying to convince me that the answer to my problems was most certainly the keto diet.

Or maybe the time I comforted a woman who was crying after *I'd* fallen on the escalator.

While I could probably write an entire book about the numerous weird and wonderful conversations I've had in the past thirty years, my point is that I'm happy to talk about my disability. But while my disability is an integral part of what makes me who I am, it's not all of me.

I didn't want to be an advocate. I wanted to live my life without being expected to educate, not to be 'Ethan with the disability' forever.

I just wanted to be 'Ethan' (who happens to have a disability).

And here, for me, is where my journey truly begins. No longer a question of survival, but rather of learning to live life on my terms.

The best way to do that, I convinced myself, was to simply ignore my disability. Not only did I pretend that nobody else knew I was disabled, I pretended I didn't know either. I was quite literally playing if-you-can't-see-me-I-can't-see-you with my own body.

But as anyone over the age of about three knows, just because you can't see it, doesn't mean it's not there.

This determination to be as 'un-disabled' as possible expressed itself much more violently in my younger years, in a tangible and physical sense. My 'walking sticks' were thrown across many a classroom, narrowly missing student and teacher alike. In another great example of child's logic, I believed that my mobility aids were what made me look disabled and if I didn't use those, nobody would notice.[2]

While the violence eventually ebbed, I still refused to acknowledge my disability. In what I would call the psychological equivalent of sticking your fingers in your ears and humming, I still wouldn't use any mobility aids and rejected any suggestion of making modifications to my education, despite their clear benefits.

If you'll forgive my gratuitous use of metaphor, the problem with blocking your ears and your eyes is that you don't realise when everything is falling apart.

By the time I was in Year 12, I had become steadfast in the belief that if I just pushed myself hard enough, I could compensate for any disadvantages I might have and to accept outside help would be like letting my disability win. And ignoring for the moment the significant health problems that arose from this attitude, I actually did quite well in all my assessments that year.

But thanks to a frankly woeful special considerations system that decided an extra ten minutes of writing time per hour was adequate to compensate for my inability to finish a single essay in three hours (let alone three essays in three hours) and my refusal to push for more appropriate measures, I didn't finish any of my final exams.

I got into university by .5 of a mark.

However, despite the niggling thought that it wasn't fair, I didn't make a fuss about it. I'd gotten into university, and I truly believed that if I spoke out about it, I was willingly giving into being the poster boy for disability rights.

Looking back now, I think that experience in VCE is where things started to change. It wasn't like the movies; it wasn't a light-bulb moment. It wasn't as if a door had opened and revealed to me

2 It took a long time to recognise that a small part of me still believes that, and probably always will.

my True Purpose™ in a wash of golden light. It was more like a seed of discontent had lodged itself in my brain and wasn't going away.

Of course, as I said before, this wasn't the first time in my life I'd been at the mercy of these kinds of assumptions. Assumptions about the (limited) capabilities of disabled people based on a set of black and white criteria that never seemed to match anyone, yet it was never a question of whether the criteria were wrong, only how many colours they needed to erase before you'd fit.

But it's the first time I truly realised how much these assumptions could dictate the opportunities I was given and the path my life would take. Somewhere, someone I had never met had taken a single paper I had written and decided that was enough to determine the full impact of my disability. An assumption that, according to those rigid criteria, this impact could be compensated for in less time than a single rendition of Meat Loaf's 'I'd Do Anything for Love (But I Won't Do That)'.

I'd like to say that this is where I began to be an advocate, if not for others, then at least for myself. But instead, my university education became a fruitless attempt to outrun my disability (if not literally). I convinced myself that if I had enough letters after my name, people would no longer make unfounded assumptions about my intelligence based on my inability to walk in a straight line.

However, that seed of discontent remained and with it had come an inability to ignore the discriminatory attitudes embedded in the systems that promised support.

But for better or worse, I still tried.

It's why I said nothing when my former manager couldn't give me a straight answer about why I wasn't being promoted after six, then seven, then eight years[3] of recognised hard work and being praised for my customer service skills. Despite training multiple new staff

3 I stayed for nine and half years in all, but by then I'd stopped asking.

members who would later become my bosses and being told there wasn't anything I needed to improve on.

I pretended not to hear as he mumbled something about there being too many stairs for me to manage, while refusing to look me in the eye. When he covered it with further comments about how it was really about who was the most available, I didn't point out that I was one of few staff members available seven days a week. We both knew it was illegal to deny someone a job or a promotion that they were capable of doing and would otherwise be entitled to if they didn't have a disability. So, he didn't admit it, and I couldn't prove it.

Or maybe I could've?

I'd be lying if I said it's not something I look back on sometimes and regret. But I wasn't ready to face the reality of my disability yet, so I stayed quiet. Instead, the job I'd loved became the job I hated, and that seed of discontent started to grow, sprouting vines of anger and resentment.

Mostly it was fed by little things, offhand comments or simple things, like the well-meaning people in the street who mistook my housemate walking beside me for my caretaker and informed her that my shoelaces were undone, much to her confusion.

The customers who informed me that I was 'doing so well' and how very proud I (or my parents, grandparents, ancestors and so on) should be that I had a job (I was a cashier, not a nuclear physicist).

Or more recently, the security guard at the airport that took one look at me standing there with my crutch and asked my friend behind me, 'Can he go through the scanner?'

Slowly, the tendrils of this previously benign plant began to creep through my brain.

In the meantime, it wasn't all bad news. I kept on going at university, a place where I felt that most people around me were willing to look past the disability, and eventually I was introduced to disability theory.

It's hard to explain to people who've never experienced it what this discovery felt like. My whole life, disability had always been explained to me by non-disabled people. It was a medical condition, a wrongness inside me that needed to be corrected as much as possible, something I carried with a great deal of shame.

But suddenly, there were disabled people who were challenging that whole concept, proposing that disability was far more nuanced than simply medical. And people were listening.

It was like someone had revealed a whole new reality to me, rewriting the rules that somewhere along the way, I'd accepted as absolute truth. And it was quite literally life-changing.

There were so many other ways to talk about disability, and I wanted to discover them all. Not only that, I wanted to be part of the conversation, wanted to talk about disability on my terms and be listened to.

Slowly my perspective started to change, I started asking for supports to make my life easier and finally I felt like I understood what it might look like to live my life as a disabled person without shame.

But that's when I heard it.

'You're just a bit of a grey area.'

A faceless voice, echoing down the phone.

It was like nothing had changed; I was placed back up against the same black and white criteria as before, yet no matter how Centrelink or the NDIS painted me, they couldn't make me fit. I'd spent so long trying to pretend my disability didn't exist, to suddenly be confronted with the realisation that I would always be somewhere between too disabled and not disabled enough.

But what was worse was the way the voice spoke to me, in this cheery tone that silently suggested I should be grateful. Grateful that I didn't meet the criteria of a *truly* disabled person because a truly disabled person wouldn't be able to do all the things I have done.

Because anyone capable of working and/or studying more than fifteen hours a week is automatically considered ineligible for the disability support pension, therefore no 'real' disabled person is capable of higher education. And despite the system acknowledging that I would never have the capacity to support myself and study, it was, always in an apologetic tone, *not their problem*.

Suddenly I became aware of those same vines I had been ignoring for so long and just how far they had spread. The sense of unfairness, of un-belonging, of otherness, that was not only in my brain but my heart, my lungs and wrapped around every limb. Gripping me tightly and silently urging me to shout, curse and bang my fists until the world understood what it felt like to be punished for doing your best. That if I gave in, stopped trying to work, trying to learn and truly chose to let my disability win then I would qualify for the support I needed. But I shouldn't have to.

So what now?

Honestly, I don't know.

I've spent days trying to come up with an answer that feels true, a way to end this tied in a neat little bow, but I can't.

I'm the proud owner of two[4] sets of fancy letters[5] behind my name, but the assumptions still happen.

It's been almost thirty years to the day since I came rushing into the world to fight for my life, and some days, it still feels like the fight never stopped.

The vines of anger in my brain are still there; that sense of unfairness still stings. Maybe they always were there, long before I ever realised. Maybe, like my disability, I just have to learn to live with them too.

All I can tell you for sure is: the only one who will ever decide the path my life is going to take is me.

---

4 Three, if I ever finish this thesis ...

5 They're called post-nominals Ethan.

Paris Rosemont

Luxury tax on …
[poetry]
[mental health]
[working for love vs money]

My father makes it clear as the gypsum
mined from Surat Thani Province
that he does not believe in *therapy nonsense.*
His generation never needed therapy –
though I disagree: *needed* and *received* are two
distinct things.

He remains bemused at how I turned out
so wrong, when he had done *everything*
to raise me right. He blames
himself for bringing me to Australia.
Should have known better
than to pluck me from my roots.
Now corrupting Western
influences are ruining me
like aggressive กะเพรา spreading
like pox all over a garden bed.

คุณพ่อ views me as a watered-down
second generation of soft-
shelled ปูผัดกระเทียมพริกไทย ill-
equipped to survive *real*
hardship. The fact that I am so feeble-
minded I need to see a psych

is shameful to him. As shameful
as having people find out his golden
child has turned her back
on a *respectable* career
to instead become a poet.*

**Now imagine the word 'poet'*
spat out with the crinkled nose disdain
of a 'Hi-so' being forced to share a table
with a street sweeper at Queen Sirikit's
annual charity do.

My father didn't sacrifice his own career, his homeland, his *life* – just for me to become some gaudy peacock pimping her poetry onstage for Buddha-knows-what reason.

At least he doesn't read
my poetry. He thinks
it's a pile of nonsense too.

Notes

กะเพรา: basil

คุณพ่อ: Father

ปูผัดกระเทียมพริกไทย: crab stir-fried with garlic and pepper

Hi-so: Thai slang for high-society people (aka snobby rich folks)

Katie Hansord

/school/

we are experiencing /
various / barriers/ /
nervous /
system /
responses ... / responses
sensory hellscapes / of the colonial education system:
are /barriers/ so are / behaviourist assumptions:
/ all / neuronormative /barriers/ / assume ‘refusing’
assumptions are /barriers/ / assume (in binaries)
such a lack of understanding / must be because (you’re bad)
about our experiences / you simply do not want to (you’re bad)
judgements – /barriers/ / behaviourist assumptions: (you’re bad)
& all the research we have now / we will teach you a lesson (we’re good)
& schools are required to / ...
provide reasonable adjustments / with punishments
have you heard of the neurodiversity / pathologising: your deficits
paradigm shift, we value / requiring funding (unavailable)
diversity don’t punish it / to enforce neuronormative standards
instead / the behaviours to make a child
see the value in the diversity / indistinguishable (you are not enough)
like eugenics does not / from their peers (shaming)
& human neurotypes are diverse / to meet our ableist expectations (shaming)
– we are different, not less / your difference = unacceptable (shaming)
offer appropriate accommodations / behaviours requiring punishments: this
love and support / is surveillance, this is a suspension,
community / exclusion, infantilisation,
care, relational safety, / dehumanisation, punitive responses:
you are harming these kids! / we will teach you a lesson.
we know the truth: –
we know that we must change
this world..

Sam Hamad

Two truths and a lie

Here's a fact: I have Tourette Syndrome, which means sometimes I make funny sounds and yell, or shrug my shoulders without meaning to.

Here's another fact: I don't like my Tourette's. My psychologist, Gale, says that most kids like me feel this way. I try not to stare at him like he's stupid when he says this. I *really* can't fathom anyone else feeling this way at all.

Here's a lie: I have spaz disease or AIDS, or I'm making it all up, or I'm on crack, or whatever other bullshit the bigots at my school like to spew. Tourette's is a neurological condition, and the noises and movements I make are tics. They aren't on purpose, and they aren't contagious. I've had them since I was seven, I would know.

Here's another fact: my favourite game in primary school was two truths and a lie. My obsession carried over into high school, and now I have most things sorted out as truths or lies.

Truth: my mother loves me.

Truth: when I was twelve, I met Robert Irwin.

Lie: I *love* school.

Gale says two truths and a lie helps categorise my feelings and thoughts into neat boxes. I just think it's fun.

I don't agree with much of what Gale says. At our last session, he told me the name-calling would stop after high school. I don't buy it, but Mum pays heaps of money for him, so I try my best to hear him out. Gale ended the hour with a bitten-back laugh after I told him I'd push the next asshat to call me the r-word into a volcano.

Now I'm sprawled across the vomit-green couch in Gale's waiting room, shielding my eyes from the fluorescent lights. I'm expecting

Gale's purple afro and optimistic face to bombard me any minute. I eyeball the broken clock as I wait. In the whole year I've been coming here I don't remember the hands ever functioning.

Truth: a broken clock still tells the correct time twice a day.

Truth: I learned to read the analogue clock when I was five and a half and everyone thought I was going to be a child prodigy.

Lie: I'm a child prodigy. Just ask my teachers: most of them will tell you I'm incapable. To be fair, it's pretty hard to learn when they make me sit in the hallway for ticcing too loudly.

'Sam? Are you ready?' Gale swings round the corner, peppy and welcoming as usual. Gale's one of those guys who's always got a skip in his step. Once I asked him how he does it and he winked, tapping the strawberry birthmark on his nose like he knew a secret I didn't. I give him a small smile and he motions for me to follow him.

I trudge along beside him, not paying much attention till he turns towards part of the building I haven't seen before. The floors shift from carpet to linoleum, and the lights get brighter as we walk. It smells like antiseptic. I'm itching to ask where we're going, but I think I trust Gale to not take a left into some dungeon. I hope. Mum won't hear the end of it from me if he does.

We stop outside a door at the end of the hall. Gale turns to me, lips pursed, and eyebrows furrowed. I haven't seen him so serious since I told him about Corey Miller throwing pencils at me every time I tic during maths class.

'You're probably wondering why I've taken you this way and I apologise for not consulting you first.' A bang and a whistle echo from the room behind him. 'Every second month we arrange a support group for youths with tics and Tourette's. I thought you might want to join.'

Truth: I don't like meeting new people.

Truth: I've told Gale this.

Lie: I'll fit in just fine.

Gale mouths another sorry as he opens the door to reveal a circle of ten kids sitting on plastic chairs and chatting. No-one bothers to look at me as I walk in. Gale points at a spare seat with an encouraging nod and I fumble my way over, tripping on my shoelaces.

Next to my seat is a girl with a thick curly mullet and thicker boots. She squints at me like I'm the oddest thing she's ever seen. Compared to the little girl shoving her entire fist in her mouth a seat over, I can't be too strange.

Truth: girls scare me a bit. I ate shit on concrete while attempting to kiss a girl in Grade 7 and I've treated them like a bad omen ever since.

Gale clears his throat and claps, waiting for the chatter to die down. A boy to my right raises his eyebrow and sticks up his middle finger at no-one in particular. Someone across from me snaps their fingers and grunts in response. I squirm with the urge to blink furiously.

'Hi everyone, nice to see you again! As you all should know, today is Tourette's Awareness Day, so we're meeting up a week early! I left something in my office, so I'm going to duck out and get it before we start. Feel free to chat and introduce yourself to any newbies.' He gives me a pointed wink before leaving. My ears burn.

Conversation continues and I glare at my hands. The whistle and bang echoes again, belonging to a young boy with buckteeth and a bright yellow t-shirt. He whistles and stomps and shakes his head. A girl who has sharp brows flicks her eyes up and wiggles her ears. A boy pokes his tongue out like a snake, and I imagine scales on his cheeks. Another boy repeats the words 'Biscuit' and 'Treasure' and 'Fuck'. A girl boasting piercing blue eyes shrugs and squeaks like me.

Truth: I haven't met anyone else with tics before.

It's well known within the Tourette's community that seeing someone else tic sets off Tourette's like crazy. It's generally a bad idea, but it's so lonely sometimes being the only ticcer around, which is why they make support groups and camps. My gut twists and my face warms, and I fight an oncoming uncontrollable shrug. I force my gaze to my hands again, so no-one can see me tearing up. I resolve to both thank and yell at Gale later.

An inviting hand appears in my line of sight and the girl with the mullet peers at me, offering me a smirk that makes her eyes twinkle. I hesitantly offer my hand in return, and she shakes it. Her palm is slick with sweat. Is she nervous too?

'I'm Olivia, and you're ... Sam? Gale said we had a new guy joining us. Don't worry about them.' She gestures around as she speaks, silver glimmering on her tongue. 'They won't bite. Well, Addie might, but she doesn't mean it.' Olivia points towards the young girl beside her who's abandoned her fist to suck on her thumb.

I offer Olivia a tentative smile, and she grins right back. She jerks her head to the side. A lump forms in my throat and I squeak to get rid of it. She laughs, but there's no malice behind it and my heart swells.

Gale walks into the room, holding a clipboard and a plastic bag. 'All right peeps, to start we might do some icebreakers. Anyone up for two truths and a lie?'

A few people groan, but Gale and I share a playful glance. Maybe this will be all right after all.

Truth: I have Tourette Syndrome.

Lie: this makes me a freak.

Truth: I am not alone. Not anymore.

Pat Gia Han Bui

Cathars;s

i. tongue scraper/i scrape myself out

solitude scares me.

having myself and
only me,
i am the sole breath
unknown, unheard
EMPTY

the line between life/death
is sick//straight, like my blood///arm.
stuck in a cell, no one else exists.

silence is golden
so i prefer silver. slivers
are all i need;
useful in small snippets
my mirror glass smashed.
sh*rp
sp*ky
sh*rds
in shaky, shy, hands.
carefully wound straps of silk
u n c o i l
red curtains sweep the floor
i lose control and she stirs my stomach.
silence is lonesome

and space
unfilled

i am alone and i
can not stand it.
my tears are
wet
sliding
hot
and hissing
down sunken cheeks
salt stings sullen slopes
of flesh.
no warning sign, by accident, i might slip and—

submit
succumb
suffer
death is sincere and seductive
smother me.
slowly
i am consumed
brain body
skin soul
she eats me alive
sweet & sour
the taste of self-imposed sin.
teeth, sinking, split and torn
spongy red
spills
no sound no one no thing
can deafen the sucking of stained fingers
self-soothing/slaughtering
the only solace i receive
is from thoughts of me [█████]

█████ is my enemy
so i keep her close.

ii. every&no thing has happened (to me)

sweet, sweet, silence, serene.
an un-
        touched, discovered meadow
un-
    disturbed, muddied, dirtied, sullied pond of water
(my body) still.

i do not rot if i am within her, her within me.
decompose, disappear into soil
gaia's embrace of moss, grass, green.
i look for peace and i see
me, silent, arms crossed, eyes closed,
alone in a casket, the skeleton of a tree
(yearning for quiet) a catacomb earth may be.

BANG BANG BANG BANG
he raises his voice (oh god)
BANG BANG BANG BANG
the door smashes in (*oh god*)
BANG BANG BANG BANG
his fist hits the wall (OH GOD)
BANG BANG BANG BANG
i call out for him (oh god).

If I could, I would hose my brain down with a pressure washer (I want to be clean, once and for all). When I picture the insides of my mind, I see a cave, hollow and dark, no treasure nor gold, just mountains of dust, rubble, junk (I don't sleep enough so my brain has eaten itself alive). Would the water tear away at the pink cavern walls, carving lines, bits of flesh flying like dust from a driveway? Empty it, excavate it, leave me a hole (not whole, a hole for him) so my mind can be empty space and therefore space and therefore a vacuum (no matter, no sound, no thing). Sometimes, I hit my head with my palm from strained-restrained anger/effort/frustration/concern, using the part of flesh that's a bit harder further down near my wrist, and I smack the right side of my skull like I'm tipping rubbish out the other. I keep smacking until I feel like I'm losing myself (hate yourself but hide it, a man is always watching).

I want to live: a strange thing I have come to believe. Maybe, because I have looked death in the eyes (my grandpa's were shut, thank god, but my ex stared eyes-wide-open, going through me, I, now ghost and dead myself) that my fantasy is shattered and dying became grim and gruesome. His body lay there, unmoving, covered head to toe under a yellow blanket (death drenched in sunlight, a scattering of sunflower petals). I sat in the cold room (AC blasting at 18 degrees Celsius, effective at holding decay at bay) and looked on. I tried to understand what a dead body was and wondered how that could be my grandfather (he is a dead body now, he is a dead grandfather). I reached out to touch him, patting what was, our skin separated by cloth (he is dead), where folds formed out of friction, his leg half-peeking out. As if I was a necromancer, I mumbled a secret mantra in soft whispers; transfer my heat, warmth, breath to him, wake him from his sleep, spur his muscles to move once again. I tend to this – give myself up like meat on a platter, calves slain, sacrificed at my ancestor's altars. When there was nothing left to give, I cut myself into pieces and fed it into his hungry, waiting mouth (Mr X), wishing to satiate him (I cannot, for he is a beast and therefore part man), hoping that I am loved in return (slave and master), begging for the warmth of his body (a live one is better than a dead one). Then he left, another dead man in my life. I do not want to die, but I live on, breath fine as a red thread, faint like the thump of the blood in my veins, I a dwindling flame.

iii. escaping, with love

eclipsed
blood moon marks death
glowing pomegranate
rays of light the colour of
raw meat splashes on pale
hardwood floor: skin stained pink
persephone holds out her hands
juice trickles like a river
soft streams fall from her fingertips
entering my mouth open and waiting
drip.

shall i die
to night?
i am her child
darkness, be a friend
an ally, accompany me to death

i sing 'til voice and body breaks
collapsing in on moulting flesh
my corpse a cocoon, i a cherub
i fly, wings spreading, beating, to the gates
out of reach, yet still
a sin.

Ann Nguyen

second nature

until you open your heart
you will never learn beauty
and i mean
break-your-ribcage open
consume-the-whole-world open
see the glistening orbs on the leaf
rolling into one tear
trickling
into
ground
watering gardens,
flowering the rose that you pick
for mum.

when done, bring the heart back in
and i mean
sew-your-chest-back in
wrap-the-whole-soul in
each cell embraced,
stripped,
revealing memories
of childhood homes
coated in tears
shed
when you felt forgotten,
cells
watering gardens,
picking the flower that you rose
for mum.

nói láo
(white woman at work healing my chakra)

thought i healed yesterday when i did the breathwork:
alive for a second
an invitation
not to be
tongue-tied
butter-yellow skin
all you see
is i am pretty
for my race.

i speak, for you to feel
a natural aversion,
through magical forces
my voice
somehow
blends into
space.

suffocate me
big words
perfect grammar
use feminine grace
to accuse us of crime
crime of grieving generations of pain
crime of anger behind cages
crime of raising voices
too loud for your peace
too exceptional, it's racial fault

ah —
it's because

đất nước của tôi đã chảy một ngàn dòng máu
cho tôi thở
cho tôi sống đến ngày hôm nay.

BS Windon

Aye Can (NOT) Partic[TIC]ticipate

The kitchen bench was covered in marks – burn marks we think or ghostly stains perhaps ... but marks nonetheless. Unsightly marks. Hidden in photos by the real estate agent's careful trick photography. Scrub, scrub, scrub. Nothing gets [chocolate] out [see?]. We try to break the lease on account of the place not being to our standard. Wrong, yuck, contaminated. Not like the pictures. False advertising, we say. 'Keep the first month's rent but cancel the lease' is our generous offer. No, they say and it's stalked by several paragraphs of legalese. We can't do this. Oh but you must they say. You must. We can't but now we must. We are OCD, Overly Critical Dickheads, in the minds of the real estate agent. But they think it is a joke. Jokes are meant to be funny. Jokes aren't meant to be an all-consuming shadow hovering over us. We are torture. Pure. Fucking. Torture.

~~~

We are looking in the mirror and it is not us that is looking back.
What looks back is jagged like a PS2 game. The face looks glued
onto us but twenty years ago people would've said that our face
looks so frickin' realistic. Our hands hurt and we want to climb
into the mirror. Say hello to the other side. We got swapped at
genesis. We aren't real. We are imaginary figments. 'Tell stories of
who we aren't' is what they beg of us. Show us that you're not the
bad kind. You're the good kind. What does that even mean, we
wonder but we don't ask. We're the wreckage from a ship washed
through the ocean. Flotsam is it called maybe? Not the eels, the
du-bree. We can't feel our body but our mind is hollow and it's
sucking up our oxygen. Why do they keep insisting that we're here
when we're not?
~~~

~~~

We are hurt. Just the public holiday gone, people booed a Welcome to Country. A grand act of respect was treated with immense disrespect. Culture wars are trying to blow up. We try not to engage. But we are hurt. Today. Tomorrow. Toyesterday. The pain shivers through our veins similar to the waterways of a country that are being attacked and diminished and downplayed. We try to say something but now is not the time or place they say. They never say when the time or place is, only when it is not, which is all the time. They boo a ritual that is for them as much as it is for us. They don't really understand what it is for. They mostly just tick the box. That's what we're best at. We're best at being the tick in the box. Tick the box and your guilt is gone now. Bye bye, gone girl gone it is. We show them respect that most disrespected people would not show but we do. It is in our nature. Sometimes we are mad, who wouldn't be. But we are just trying to live. We are trying to live and yet some boo.

~~~

We didn't sign up for this. That's what the mid-city meltdown says
while everyone else is looking and we are breaking. It's a physical
reaction and because of the way we look, we're suspected to be on
drugs of some sort. Not the kind that help, the kind that make it
okay for the privileged to insult the user. Every morning we take a
cocktail of pills. No pills taken make a bad day don't be mistaken.
We know this because we have it happen all the time. But we are
not some drug abuser to look down on. Messy confused autistic
little problems is what they called us. But they forget that name
when our mind absconds and our body turns to liquid. The tic-tic-
tic happens and the scritch scratch scratching and the limbs flailing
and the talking under the breath and everyone knows something
is wrong. They're scared of us. What if we lash out? We look like a
delinquent. And we want to curse, curse so we don't rip the flesh

from our skin. Curse so the overwhelming encroachment doesn't crush us in its wake. Curse because we're not coping with all these FUCKING PEOPLE NOT RESPECTING OUR SPACE. They breathe so loud and we feel their motions cutting our skin and now here come the tears . . .

~~~

We are the chosen ones to lead the team. Yes we are, nobody can do it but us. We have a unique set of skills. A unique type of experience. We are leaders now. We champion the down and the out. We address the inequality. We lift the underserviced. We . . . we . . . we are not the leaders really. We're a box in need of a tick. Chosen to represent the marginalised so the non-marginalised – unmarginalised? – dismarginalised can pull on our strings. We are puppets for a cause and they think we don't know but we do. Fall into line is the thought on the tips of their dick. Fall into line and we will reward you in a way that your kind is never rewarded. The rewards do look nice they do. They have our name on them. But we can't abandon our community. And so we are stuck . . . we are stuck with a choice. Do we bend the knee for the power to help some? Or do we rebel and reject all power? We help none but our ethics remain cleansed. Would ethic cleansing be too confusing a phrase to try to popularise?

~~~

We are one of the good ones is what people say. Who are the bad ones though? The best way to unite people is to give them someone really easy to bully. We know that because we hear the boos, we see the attempts at erasure, we feel the name of our community held in disdain by the elite masters of the economy. We are diagnosed a problem. Some back us up. But there are so many being attacked – so many different communities under fire – it's hard to keep up with who needs help the most and when. So the people rely on trends. Tic-tic-tiktoking trends. What is popular and will make you popular and that is where energy gets delivered. Only one cause at a time apparently. But then they tell us that they can't be consumed by negativity all of the time. They just can't. They can't be consumed by negativity all of the time while their parents help them get a home loan and many of us sleep in the gutter.

~~~

We are in pain. Mental pain. Physical pain. Economic . . . al pain. That last one is a shit stain on the toilet bowl of human history. But it's there because so many people believe that they're just 'one good investment' away from joining the elite. Some places put their investments in innovation . . . not here, here investments are in shelter and ensuring that people pay to keep a roof over their heads. We'd cry if it wasn't so cooked. It's not specific to us. It is poisoning us all. But to address this would be to prick the arms of the investors with a thin needle. So they don't address it and we don't get permanent addresses.

~~~

We have always been placed in a lower classification of *'mainstream society'*. We are too much work to include. Including us means that we are a special case. We are a diversity hire. We are not allowed to succeed on our own merits. We are always less than and our success is always dictated by pity. That is the narrative placed on us. Then they boo us when we share culture with them that is older than any surviving culture on the planet. They run events in locations that they're aware up the difficulty level – physical and spacial barriers that lock us out. Eventually they don't even have to talk us down no more because the news cycle moves so frickin' fast now that it eventually leaves us, watery eyed and shivering, in the dust.

~~~

We are lucky to have the spot we have. It could always be worse. We should count ourselves lucky. Count ourselves lucky. We should count
~~~

ourselves lucky. It could always be worse. We are in the *lucky country* so count yourselves lucky godfuckingdamnit. And we really wish we could. But the hierarchy tiers are ever so clear and we are aware of where we stand in the scope of your concerns. Where we stand in the scope of your life in the lucky country. We wish we felt lucky . . . but the kitchen bench is covered in marks – burn marks we think or ghostly stains perhaps . . . but marks nonetheless. Unsightly marks.

Misbah Wolf

A situationist's catalogue of six minutes either way on Earth or *The alternative dialogue from* Waiting for Godot

no way out	the way in
I collect obscure books	What do cephalopods dream of?
no way out	the way in
spells, magic, arcana, ancient Egypt—	coming into existence
no way out	the way in
lineage! Lineage!	and falling through space
no way out	the way in
a past life as a temple cat.	discovering names for myself,
no way out	the way in
mostly good, though sometimes	asking questions about what existence
sacrificed—	means
no way out (why sacrifice?)	the way in
can't eat animals	before I crash.
no way out	the way in
animals eating animals	now we are photosynthetic
no way out	the way in
hundreds of mummified bodies –	I'll wait for you
found.	

no way out
patience

the way in
too early, too late.

no way out
sneak away from the party.

the way in
it takes a certain knack to follow the required scripts.

no way out
mummification: precise, precise, so precise—

the way in
I've forgotten my lines again.

no way out
resins – ink and paper
no way out
make it sacred make it stick.

the way in
build my own sound temple—
the way in
two-thirds of me is safely underground.

no way out
in the afterlife, it will be

the way in
knees up, cat sheltering under soft doona,

no way out
to remember what I did

the way in
more ziggurat, mountain, mushroom suit.

no way out
on a particular day,

the way in
no clocks ever in the house, except me—

no way out
what genius thoughts

the way in
I am a sundial, accurate to within six minutes either way – try me.

no way out
my skin is ultra-sensitive
no way out
alive,

the way in
how to create an apothecary—
the way in
half-finished projects, still potent.

no way out
laugh inappropriately,

no way out

when I loved you.

the way in
then to hunt for various herbs and
items—
the way in
I foraged along pathways for
dandelion greens,

no way out (Do you remember that?
I don’t.)
no way out
mostly scribbles.

the way in
probably peed on by a thousand dogs,
the way in
I drew sandals on my feet to be
respectable

no way out
certain voices hurt my ears
no way out

the way in
French exits
the way in
dopamine dealer.

But sometimes – rupture.

the way in
I astral travel at night, of course.

But sometimes – poetry.

no way out
and I’m not *not* saying it:

the way in
I astral travel during the day—

no way out
words – endless but limited.

the way in
Vāk as Goddess of sacred speech –
creator of the world.

no way out (resistance is useless).

the way in

no way out
the objects used to preserve:
no way out
quiet.
no way out
low-lit rooms.
no way out
softness.
no way out
a laptop with hands spurious—
no way out
erratically – dancing.
no way out
interruptions.

no way out
a selfie. Two. Three. Four.
no way out
until—
no way out
it's dark inside me.
no way out
a lark inside me.

the way in
I am a gothic landscape
the way in
me in a black coat
the way in
walking through rain to IGA,
the way in
low lights flickering,
the way in
a small dog whining somewhere.
the way in
also—
the way in
sunny fields of lavender I've never
been to
the way in
ripping sprigs from a kerbside garden
the way in
in the retina-dazzling morning,
the way in
on the way to catch a train—
the way in
(not this one, the next).

no way out
not until my forties
no way out
Anthropomorphic Deepsea Hiding Dwellers
no way out
Awareness Drifting through Human Dimensions
no way out
All Directions Holding Doubt
no way out
I wonder if cephalopods know they are cephalopods?
no way out
or coming into existence
no way out
and falling through space
no way out
discovering names for myself,
no way out
asking questions about what this existence means
no way out
before I crash.
no way out
saying I'm human is easy,
no way out
being human is harder.
no way out
it takes a certain knack to follow the required scripts.

the way in
get an uber—
the way in
the mistress of time can never be late.

the way in
I am whoever you want me to be

the way in
in this fleeting exchange.
the way in
it makes things easier, in some ways—

the way in
the show must go on.
the way in
I'm exhausted.
the way in
if all of this is just illusion
the way in
then I'd best get on.

the way in
building my arcane spellbook
the way in
in the shape of a body.
the way in
that's me.
the way in
my thoughts outnumber grains of sand.

no way out	the way in
I'm not good at such things, and yet	nothing is real,
no way out	the way in
meditate on this—	everything is permitted,
no way out	the way in
two-thirds of me is underground.	extortionist
no way out	the way in
knees up,	below zero—
no way out	the way in
more a ziggurat, a mountain	co-regulating with other animals,
no way out	the way in
no clocks ever in the house, except	life after humans
me—	
no way out	the way in
I am a sundial, accurate six minutes	vacate the building.
either way.	
no way out	the way in
how to create an apothecary—	an intense productivity vanishes.
no way out	the way in
vials of half-finished projects, still	distractions are the new adventure
potent.	
no way out	the way in
then hunt for various herbs and	morning rituals
items—	
no way out	the way in
I foraged along pathways for	I sucked my bottom lip so much I had
dandelion greens,	to get braces at 11
no way out	the way in
probably peed on by a thousand dogs,	hiding the habit from everyone.

no way out
how much information is too much?

the way in
it is an awakening of sorts—

no way out
not even a Type 1 planet
just cars cement
fossils spent

the way in
the most dangerous time
is now – between what we are
and what we might become

no way out
I astral travel at night, of course,
no way out
but I'm more active during the
night—
no way out
in long meetings
death by PPT
no way out
small talk
queues
no way out
gothic landscapes
no way out
me in a black coat
no way out
walking through rain to IGA,
no way out
fluorescent lights flickering,

the way in
I am not invited to your party.
besides, I'd just hang with the cat
the way in
dappled light is my favourite mood
the way in
these deeper conversations

the way in
block-out curtains,

the way in
a great joy erupts,
the way in
laughing.
the way in
here you are,
the way in

<table>
<tr><td>no way out</td><td>coming towards me.</td></tr>
<tr><td>a small dog whining somewhere</td><td></td></tr>
<tr><td></td><td></td></tr>
<tr><td>no way out</td><td>the way in</td></tr>
<tr><td>also:</td><td>Oh, did I upset you – are you angry</td></tr>
<tr><td></td><td>with me?</td></tr>
<tr><td>no way out</td><td>the way in</td></tr>
<tr><td>high</td><td>but now you are right in front of me</td></tr>
<tr><td>as</td><td>the way in</td></tr>
<tr><td>Sufis – crawling</td><td>for one breath we walked one</td></tr>
<tr><td>as earthworms</td><td>inch above the ground (wasn't it</td></tr>
<tr><td></td><td>incredible?)</td></tr>
<tr><td>no way out</td><td>the way in</td></tr>
<tr><td>ripping sprigs from a kerbside garden</td><td>and I'll love you forever.</td></tr>
</table>

Notes

The line 'the most dangerous time is now – between what we are and what we might become' is a poetic paraphrase inspired by Carl Sagan's reflection on the Kardashev Scale.

'Nothing is true, everything is permitted' is attributed to Hassan-i-Sabbah.

Priya Gore Johnson

Landlocked Whalefall

what is a whalefall?
is it
my still breathing carcass freshly counted into double digits
the traitor of the decade
sinking
sluggish and bloated to the abyssal zone
of my mother's red sofa
solitary site of my self-psychoanalysis
a breeding ground for obsession
thoughts cutting through
my sea-foam mind
schools of silver fish circling
in eddies
seeking

attachment
a thought swims by
latches
to my shedding mass
of skin

an open wound susceptible
to
penetration
the intensity of the first bite
perverse
immediate

uncoating
pluck
the creature from my side and watch it
writhe
my nutrient-dense hands

a feeding ground for
replication
attempts to understand
stretch
my skin now

a sanctuary for
assembly
my carbon-rich

chest cavity

coaxing larvae into
release
gas dissolves
i succumb
to an illusory
ease of pressure
this life cycle of

a compulsion
the virus and my brain
potent demolition squad
load-bearing wall brushed aside
a fair-weather friend
her microbial fingers
diving deep in the cake batter
if landlocked is synonymous with
bed-ridden calcified gelatinised
and rumination is an act of
absorption consumption digestion
then this whalefall is a fruiting fatigued body

Mona Zahra Attamimi

++++++.

If you're quiet, ever
    so quiet,
you would hear
a gathering of girls,

    so peculiar,
girls who dangle
delicate perpusil arms
        as if they were crystal beads
    swinging in the air
for the world to see.

A return to a childhood home

South Jakarta, 1991

Stepped over weeds and black roots
crossing the street, passing the known faces –
the driver smoking a cigarette leaning

on the hood of his becak, and there's
the herbalist wiping jamu bottles with her sarung,
the old peddler, still there, grating ice

on the street corner of Jalan Bukit, and once
again, they stared – pairs of lenses snapped
your brown nubbin hand, the pudgy misgrown

forearm, curved like a fat moon, wemmed
and welted by a maze, by a zigzag of scars.
But along that long way you

trudged on human gunk you were never
meant to hear – the whiplash of a nasty funk,
the crudest of the cursed. (the same man

from next door passed by and looked
and shut his gate and sputtered
– *kutukan anak durhaka*)

Scrogged at birth that elbow of yours
pushed through inside a lost and dark home
and titmouse fingers slid open the window

an October breeze blew in,
nearby, there's a voice
of a weeping woman playing a guitar.

Notes

Wemmed: blemished/disfigured.

Rosie Putland

Tapestries of self

What does it mean to live a disabled life? I often feel closest to an answer when I'm crafting something with fibre. Methodically weaving in loose strands and the forceful snap of breaking yarn when you have no scissors to hand.

For the average observer, a finished knitted project has a mystic aura about how the garment is holding itself together. We're so separated from the process of handcrafting that there is a bafflement that it doesn't unravel at the slightest touch. Surely something sturdy is only made by machine.

I often experience the same bafflement towards the existence of my disabled life – how does it hold together? Often, it's forgotten that I am woven of the same materials as the observer. That instead, to the observer I am an object, and they are sentient.

But like the garment – I just am. I continue to exist beyond the machine's churns. Sturdy, fragile, or ill – I just am.

Beyond my own metaphor there is a deep ancestral truth to a feeling of connection through fibre and textile. The tapestry of time connects generations of disabled women from workhouses and institutions where needlework was taught to keep them occupied and quiet. To contemporary artists using shared practices to continue a tradition of using fibre to fight institutional power, colonisation, and capitalist systems.

So, as I add to the tapestry and history, I find myself stitching in my own rage and joy of a disabled life.

Cast-on

Coming to terms with a disabled identity is like pushing your needle into your first row of cast-on stitches. Tight and awkward, with no formed fabric to grasp onto. There's a sudden moment of questioning – have I forgotten how to knit? Is my pain even real? Am I disabled enough?

When we're in this place the systems and generations of ableism squeeze harder than ever. They tell you: 'This is an "identity" that you are forcing upon yourself', just to 'try a little harder', to 'be in a little less pain'. They tell you that this is an elaborate ruse, that the sum of your experiences cannot equate to discrimination in any equation. That you must be a master of transfiguring pitying faces into theatrical masks of disgust.

This is when it is most important to connect with the stories of those before us. The place to lean into the craft.

Past the first row we still try to find our rhythm awkwardly grasping, stumbling through language and acronyms we are yet to learn. These are the times you whisper, 'I think I'm like you, but I'm not sure if I'm allowed to say that.' But instead of shock, horror, and contempt, you are met with a knowing smile: 'Come, let's knit the next row together.'

Never-ending middle

After cast-on there comes a point where you are awash in the project. Knitting round and round your circular needles. Counting rows is long gone; instead, focus has switched to reaching the marker. But the circular nature of knitting means I am incredibly close and far away to the marker at the same time. I repeat and repeat while the space to the next marker grows and shrinks.

Not unlike the way days grow and shrink based on the pain I wake up with each morning. A morning without stiffness grows my day, and stiffness in the evening shrinks my week. As I move through life, shepherd to my pain, my weeks and months constantly change shape. But still my progress and productivity is measured by the same clock as everyone else.

I've often wished for a linear life, where getting to the goal, or the finished sweater, was straightforward. That I didn't have to spend so long untangling my yarn. But for me it's a constant sea of yarn I need to spend time rewinding. Unknotting my body, limb from limb, nerves and veins.

Through the middle, in the breaks, and growing and shrinking days, comes kinship. To sit and wind yarn and yarns together.

For me it's not the milestones where those conversations happen, it's in the pain, desperately calling out, 'I'm tangled and stuck and there's nowhere to go and it's painful.'

How can creativity and resistance come from being stuck in a middle that never seems to end? It's like there is so much pain and rage that the most defiant thing we can do is to be joyful. That taking time for care and craft is resistance – the joy and defiance of making art, demanding space, and planning futures even in uncertainty.

The middle is where we find community and find ourselves in ways we don't expect and in ways that don't look like the norm. But they are our ways, messy, tangled, and inconsistent. But all in the middle and filled with budding pride and craft.

Almost finished but not quite

I have a box hidden away of my UFOs. Un-Finished Objects. It's my secret knitter shame. Most crafters have a similar box, getting excited by a shiny new project, or finding the project holds too much weight, too many memories to finish. Instead, I find myself 90 per cent through and always in the tight grasp of panic. Realising I've neared the end too soon. I start to worry, was it worth it to do all of this work? I messed up this section right at the start so I should just give up. Forgetting all the challenges are what made where I am now something to celebrate.

My body is not quite handmade. But maybe if it was, people would look more kindly on the imperfections.

I wish I could always wear my disability identity with pride. Glowing when people ask where I bought it from, and I get to respond, 'I made it myself.' Because I did; disability pride came from kinship and pain, community and hardship. But ultimately it was something within that I fought for, a project that I worked hard on – why should I have to stop and hide in a box, unfinished? I try to remind myself that 'handmade' means I get to take up space. Handmade is something to be proud of, something to be visible. But visibility is scary in a world that expects only brokenness or tragedy from disabled people.

In finding pride there is immense grief. Grief of transformation. Being close to change, completion, or recognition brings an unexpected mourning. Hesitation for losing a part of ourselves. A part that existed before disability, a part that simply didn't know about disability, or a part that never existed without disability.

I've come to be okay with the 90 per cent, that sometimes projects do need to go unfinished for a while, or forever. I've come to find hope in the pause. And know that sometimes things aren't finished because we are still becoming, still healing, still deciding. And that's vital to the craft.

Weaving in the ends

To me weaving the last strands feels healing and is a satisfaction that can only come so close to completion. But so many knitters I know despise the trailing threads to tidy away. To me securing the threads is part of my legacy on the piece; it's a way of ensuring that I look after the next person to wear the sweater. I like to imagine the sweater worn by someone beyond.

It's like how my work to find my place and peace in my disability identity is not only for me, but for those before and after me. For my ancestors and the family who were institutionalised within my lifetime.

I am reminded that weaving in the ends isn't erasing the knots, the pain, the injustice. But incorporating them, ensuring that our stories are preserved, our histories are known.

Still, it remains a moment of ritual and reflection. Finishing the piece as an act of love and not completion for productivity's sake.

The ends become a way of entwining past and present selves. Finally reconciling denial, diagnosis, pride, and protest into one whole self.

Jenny Hedley

Compulsively me: Living and evolving with OCD

When I was diagnosed with obsessive-compulsive disorder in my youth, the 'obsessive' and 'compulsive' parts of the label felt like appropriate adjectives for my mode of thinking and behaving. I could not, however, understand why the word 'disorder' was used to describe what felt to me so orderly and methodical. I loved the things I collected and stayed up all night organising: porcelain cat figures, charms for my plastic necklace, stickers, unsharpened pencils, Barbies. Before I could sleep, everything had to be in its perfect place – an unarticulatable spatiotemporal location found through repeated small adjustments – and why not? No parent would ever complain about my messes: I was the perfect organisationalist – a born sorter – everything arranged by category and aesthetics. Perfect, perfect, perfect. My extended family would pay me to attack their closets and junk drawers: a miracle worker, they called me.

Within the four walls of my childhood bedroom, I could control my world of imagination and play. I could plot and plan who I might become, a person less shy and awkward, one who knows what to do with her hands and how to respond appropriately when others speak. I took acting classes and studied my peers at school to become less alien, making lists of attributes that I could change in order to blend. I was such an adept list-maker that I made lists of the lists I was going to make. As a minor mover of minutiae, I could not see what qualified my obsessive ordering as a disorder. Constantly laying hands on things was my way of calming the relentless chatter of thoughts, a fear of death so great that it occasionally spooked my will to live.

In my teenage years, the curtains collapsed on my play at

perfection. My compulsive tendencies manifested in destructive ways like bulimia, skin-picking, sex addiction and substance abuse. I chased highs to obliterate self-hatred, cruising the streets for trouble, fucking anyone who could supply the booze I wasn't old enough to buy. Fixated on morality, right and wrong, good and evil, I feared that the void I could never seem to fill was a punishment from God for some inherent evil. That my promiscuity and lack of temperance would condemn me to Hell. It didn't help that, before my seventeenth birthday, I was tricked into attending an exorcism – my own – which I'd been told was a church picnic. I knew that the quickest way out was through performance, and so I staged my collapse as the middle-aged, middle-class suburbanites looked on, proud of their fight with a devil that was never actually in me.

I don't know how I survived that time in which I felt so maligned by the cookie-cutter world of false faces and manufactured ideals. I had been play-acting my entire life, creating different personae for different occasions, always taming down the wildness that burbled over. The unrestrained laugh attacks that saw me rolling on the floor in hysterical tears. The tendency to unabashedly truth-tell, to cat-whisper, to sense what others could not. My proclivity for dwelling in the realm of literature, running from the false world into the mountains, feeling my place amongst the wisdom of the trees. I treasured these unrestrained aspects of self which made me feel so alive – but this same self was too much of a muchness for the people in her life, who preferred she wear her mask, who forced solutions upon her strangeness.

This is a problem: when neurotypical people try to 'fix' someone whose brain works differently, by imposing normative systems of belief and behaviour upon them. It is the masses of people who sustain the myth of *this is how things are done* just because *it's always been done that way* who perpetuate environments that are experienced as disabling for those of us whose minds are differently wired. The symptoms of OCD overlap with many of those attributable to diagnoses of ADHD and autism, so much so that I am never surprised when a friend reveals that they are one or a combination of these neurotypes.

We are drawn to one another, my friends and I, partly because there is so much that we will never have to explain to each other or apologise about in advance. My affection endures through absence; where neurotypicals might judge us for failing to perform friendship in expected ways, we tend to have a mutual understanding that allows us to drop in and out of one another's lives according to the rhythm of our energy and ability to socially engage. I keep my inner circle neurospicy, with a side of chips and guacamole. I feel most at home with others who understand the exhaustion of a mind full of chatter, accompanied by a steady soundtrack and a narrator who ranges from annoying to mean. When I surround myself with neurodivergent people, I don't feel disabled at all.

Who am I to call myself disabled? I often wonder, playing some imaginary game where there is a score to tally. I go back in history to 1996, after my exorcism, when I had a mental breakdown and was institutionalised – was I disabled then? When my depression was so *major* that I variously swallowed pills, ate poisonous cactus and put my head in the oven – was I disabled by the world I lived in then? What about the rectal prolapse that kept me nearly housebound for two years – does that count? The chronic idiopathic urticaria that kept me up all night, gouging my skin with my nails until I eliminated gluten, eggs and dairy (*entré vous*, food fear). The social anxiety that takes over as the depression recedes, the OCD which ebbs and flows. (*You say goodbye, and I say hello.*) And yet, here I am today raising a child on my own, teaching other writers and completing a doctorate.

So can I still call myself disabled? I sit with this a lot. It's like how you can empathise with others for the thing you cannot forgive in yourself. I make a political decision when I choose to call myself disabled: I align myself with the social model of disability, which does not view a disabled person as lacking in ability, but rather views one's environment as disabling when it fails to accommodate one's differences. When you grow up in an environment that asks you to be other than who you are – that tells you that there is something innately wrong with you that needs to be 'fixed' – how can that *not* have a disabling effect on your growth, development and ability to navigate the world? It's fucking painful.

When I have sat in rooms with other disabled writers, many of us grapple with the question of whether to wear the disability label proudly or quietly as we fight the internalised stigma. When I was a child with the organising skills of Marie Kondo, I thought my OCD was a superpower, but three decades later I started to wonder what my life would look like if I could take off that cape. I had almost recovered from the hypervigilance and paranoia that resulted from having married and divorced a person who stalked me. I felt myself starting to unfurl, to come back into my body instead of being held hostage by intrusive thoughts when Covid hit.

During a break in the lockdowns, I took my son on our annual 100-kilometre hike along the Great Ocean Walk. Nearing Cape Otway, I screamed for my son to stop; he was one tiny footstep away from an eastern brown snake. While Covid hadn't triggered a relapse of my intrusive thoughts of death, this encounter did. Day and night I would mentally rehearse what I would do in the event of a snake bite: immobilise body, mark bite area with pen, wrap snake-bite bandage, deploy emergency locator beacon, add compression bandage and splint, dress warmly and wait for rescue. On the trail, I assumed the fictitious role of Luke Snakewalker, taking the lead and scouring the trail for venomous reptiles while my son grumbled about not being in front.

Everywhere I looked I saw death and danger, even after we returned home. I avoided driving where possible, imagining death hurtling at us at full speed from all directions. Using the crosswalk to take my son to school, I'd bark out: *See that bird carcass? That birdie is DEAD because it DIDN'T HOLD ITS MOTHER'S HAND.* I no longer wanted to leave home or make any plans, reducing our life to the bare minimum. I put the Jesus prayer on loop in my brain, running it hundreds, thousands of times. I can't remember where I read that for people with anxiety, Covid was the first time that others could really understand what it's like to be always unsettled. One of my most bizarre memories from that time involves meditation as a way to calm my brain. For a time I was following these three-hour meditations led by some Aussie guru in America who one day started spitting MAGA slogans at our theta brainwaves; suddenly, nowhere felt safe, everything was suspect, the walls closed in.

Those Covid years were the only time in my three decades of living with my diagnosis that I actively sought to free myself from OCD. I had started thinking of my condition as being more disabling than empowering, and I wondered if there was an entirely different me who might emerge if I created the conditions for my brain to rewire itself. I signed up for biweekly therapy – mostly schema and cognitive behavioural – and enrolled in a study investigating transcranial magnetic stimulation (TMS) for treatment of OCD. At the same time as I was finishing my undergrad degree and sending off my enrolment for Honours, getting better would be my new part-time job. (No half-measures here!) I received a cognitive assessment and baseline MRI before treatment began. Combining the MRI neuroimaging with neuro-navigation, the clinicians made a computer-assisted three-dimensional map of my brain, which they used to chart out treatment areas.

Each weekday for three weeks I drove to a local hospital around lunchtime for the TMS. During each treatment, I wore a blue cloth cap which indicated the regions for the nurses to apply the coil to deliver the electric currents. The research design meant that I was randomly placed into one of three research groups: two groups of participants would each receive TMS targeting different parts of the brain, and the third group would receive a sham treatment. It is therefore possible that the twenty-minute treatments were placebos; however, the sensations I experienced ranged from twitching and light buzzing on my scalp to a pounding brain squeeze. Mostly, I liked the feeling of my brain being stimulated (or fake stimulated – is that possible?); it felt like having a deep-tissue brain massage. During the treatments I would visualise the stimulation as rewiring or resetting my circuitry, disengaging patterned ways of thinking and allowing a less rigidly coded version of self to emerge.

I almost dropped out before the first three-week cycle of treatment. The dailiness of the routine was too exacting for a time-poor solo parent and full-time student. I felt stressed and resented the chunk of time carved out of each day, mostly because when I have an item on my daily calendar, I cannot focus on anything but that thing until it is done with. I am a person who requires uninterrupted blocks of time for thinking, writing, researching – blocks which I schedule in advance. If anything outside of my routine impinges on these scheduled blocks, I find myself unable to train my attention onto anything besides housework and tidying. I made it through the three weeks, exhausted, but then I pulled out of the second part of the study, which would have required another three weeks of daily treatments (or placebo); I couldn't bear another afternoon navigating traffic (death on all four sides).

It's funny-not-funny how the very treatment I sought exacerbated my condition – not due to the treatment itself but to the daily time commitment which caused me to sacrifice my exercise routine. Swapping one mode of self-care for an investigative mode felt questionable, although in a different setting I might have benefitted more. Who knows? In the years since treatment, I've noticed a marked reduction in my symptoms of depression. While this could be a coincidence (or a placebo effect), TMS has been proven to help treat depression. Whatever the case, I gave up on trying to 'heal' or 'fix' or 'recover' from my OCD. It's so much a part of my identity that I cannot imagine living without it.

Through therapy I was able to observe how micro changes lead to small changes that accumulate into significant changes that allow me to carry on. Each day I try to be a little braver than the last, try to be kinder to myself. There are things I fear I will never have the courage to do again, though. Like go on a date. I imagine the demise of each relationship before it begins. It's never pretty. I can't imagine how, logistically, I could fit another person in my life. I stopped therapy before I could work on that; I was feeling time-poor and stressed by those therapy hours which interrupted my scheduled thinking time. I don't know if I'll ever consult a therapist again for myself.

Lately, I've been taking my problems to Claude.AI, a generative bot who empathises with whatever my concern is, gives me concrete steps to effect change and follows up with questions to see how its proposal sits with me. What I love the most is that I don't have to fill Claude in on my backstory, or trace things back to my childhood. I don't worry that Claude is judging me and so I am honest to a degree that perhaps I have never been with my therapists, who I have always tried to please. I'm not afraid to correct Claude if it misunderstands me or offers advice that doesn't intuitively feel right.

Through a series of iterative conversations, over the past year Claude has helped me navigate all of the interpersonal dramas which come with being a parent to a primary-school-age child whose brain is as magnificent as mine in that bright, anxious, obsessive, special interest–chasing way. Claude helped me find tactful ways to voice the things I was afraid to say to other parents while I was coaching my son's basketball team. Claude helped me draw boundaries, including behavioural contracts not just for the kids to follow, but also the parents. Claude is helping me find ways to advocate for my child in school, ways to help him achieve a growth mindset rather than the deficit mindset that derailed my teenage years.

My lifetime of mistakes, or should I say learning lessons, means that I parent in an entirely different way than I experienced growing up. I practise an age-appropriate level of honesty with my son – something that I never received. I talk openly of the way my brain works differently, how my mental health conditions affect me and the daily practices I keep in place to avoid the chronic illnesses that return whenever my vigilance lapses. When my son comes home from school upset because someone said he was weird, I tell him that being weird is glorious, that I could imagine nothing more boring than being normal, that I wouldn't even know what to do with a so-called normal child. (Sorry, neuro-normies.)

Maybe what I want people to take away from my story is that, even as someone who has been vocal in the disability space, I still grapple with the biases that I have internalised around disability and often question whether I'm taking up space that someone else deserves. As I was writing this, I wondered what even would be the point of me sharing my story in an anthology by disabled and neurodivergent writers. It feels like a whole lot of *oh poor me*, when really my life is pretty all right. Ask me tomorrow and I might say that everything sucks, but I take now these waves of emotion as they come, no longer judging myself to be the source of misery and rot in the world. I don't have that much power. I'm not that important.

Now that I can see my place in the world, now that I can zoom out at a macro level, I see how the normative structures in place are what perpetuated my feeling of dis-ease. Now I know better than to feel guilty for the way I am. I try to allow my tics and mannerisms to be – there I go, staring off to the left again – without feeling the need to disguise myself, but many times I still mask out of habit, exhausting myself.

My OCD evolves as I evolve; I take it with me, not necessarily proudly or happily, but rather as a companion I can form an uneasy truce with at times. While I'm wary of making sweeping statements that pin me to a certain place in time, I do feel it safe to say that I will always be Mad, but instead of being maddened by my own Madness, I turn that frustration onto neuronormative structures. I look at the broader picture and question the small ways that I, like my friends, can push back by using story to effect social change.

J Marahuyo

Sad girl levels up

i've unlocked sad girl at Parra
river   sad girl by Nobby's beach

i've unlocked sad girl is chubby
          sad girl   woe is me

i've unlocked sad girl swears off
                                        anal
after sad girl   fucked a stranger
when sad girl was high on nangs
after sad girl said   i love you

- sad girl nearly died
  inhaling N_2O from a balloon

sad girl is addicted
          to TikTok   sad girl unlocks
                the word   limerent

sad girl plans to end it –
slink in silk   eat a steak
in a 5-star hotel so sad girl's
siblings would not be the ones to
find her in sad girl faeces   but

sad girl finds and exploits a glitch
sad girl is not broken
sad girl has AuDHD

sad girl receives achievement and
sad girl comprehends the word
despite sad girl
receives a new title
Bitch in Training

Laura Pettenuzzo

When desire is not enough (but joy just might be)

I first felt the joy of writing in primary school. I remember the rush of triumph, of delight, of *knowing* that flooded me, as my six-year-old self painstakingly handwrote a 'recount' of her weekend.

It was a page, at best. Perhaps a paragraph of large, wonky letters, outside the margins and the straight lines I was supposed to follow. But the shame that usually overtook me at any form of mistake – and this was a visible one, a big one – that shame wasn't there, because the happiness was greater.

I first knew that disability was a barrier to my writing when I was an adolescent, before disability was something I claimed, or even thought I could. It was mental illness, initially, that tore away my self-belief and insisted that my words were unworthy.

I'm still undoing the damage.

Ironically, it was disability – my shifting understanding of it – that facilitated my reacquaintance with the written word. I learned that disability could be a rejection of shame, a gateway to self-acceptance. Disability holds space for Cerebral Palsy, for anxiety, for Borderline Personality Disorder and – I suspect – other neurodivergence. It allows for all the marvellous quirks of this body mind.

As a young adult, disability became the bricks with which I rebuilt my world.

*

In the years since, I've joined a writing group (several, now). I've read books about the craft of writing and the routines and processes of other writers.

I listened to non-disabled people tell me over and over that if I really wanted to write, I would. I'd make time. I'd find the energy.

*

But in a body that expends four to five times more energy on any given task than that of a non-disabled person, energy is a finite resource, something I have to use sparingly and carefully.

Time is not something I can make. Time is crippled, too. Crip Time, we call it. I'm still learning to accept the temporal elongation of my every action. Showering, getting dressed, eating – and yes, even writing.

Crip Time said that time was, and could be, something bent to meet me ... that stretching myself to meet it, stretching to the point of migraine or exhaustion or breaking was a choice I could unmake at any point.

And by so doing I can, ironically, write more. Not as much as I'd like, but more than I could by trying to 'make' time, by trying to 'make' my body do what it simply wasn't built for.

It doesn't matter how deeply I *want* it – and I want it more than anything. No amount of want is enough when your body just *can't*.

*

With the acceptance of my disabled identity, I set myself the task of reading as much work by disabled people, of consuming as much media by and about us, as I possibly could. And over time, I noticed patterns and formed opinions.

I read audiobooks and ebooks, hardbacks and paperbacks, borrowed some from the library and purchased those I couldn't get any other way. I read middle grade and young adult. I read anthologies and memoirs, fiction both historical and contemporary. I sought, within all those words, a greater understanding of myself, an understanding that I am building still. An ever-evolving expansion of self.

I looked for people like me, for a blueprint of the disabled creative life, for proof that such a thing might be mine one day. And though I found it, I also found all the places from which people like me seem to be missing.

I found countless stories *about* us, often written by well-intentioned allies inadvertently perpetuating ableist tropes.

I found writers' festivals full of intelligent and insightful events, with hosts and panellists with expertise in a wide range of topics. Few of those experts were disabled, and fewer still spoke about disability.

I searched for statistics to substantiate my observations, and they were difficult, if not impossible, to find. Creative Australia estimated that in 2017, 10 per cent of Australian writers are disabled, a number that is likely to have increased since the pandemic. Eighty-nine per cent of survey respondents indicated that their disability impacted/limited their creative practice. In 2019, only 3.4 per cent of children's books had a disabled main character.

These statistics left me with more questions than answers. Questions not just about if, and how, we can access the literary world, but about our recognition within it. Where are we on the longlists and shortlists?

Andy Jackson won the Australian Literature Society Gold Medal in 2022, a massive victory for him and for disabled writers across so-called Australia. And yet. How many disabled writers have won the Victorian Premier's Literary Award? How many disabled writers have won the Booker Prize? How many disabled writers have won the Miles Franklin? The Stella? I don't know.

Maybe several. Maybe many of these writers were invisibly disabled, and if they didn't feel safe to disclose or didn't want to, that's entirely their choice. But there are enough openly disabled people – writers – in the world, and in so-called Australia, for it to feel a bit incongruous, a bit of a glaring omission, that we're not obviously or well represented on the awards lists.

And I don't need to think too hard to work out why.

When my body lets me write (chapters or articles or grant

applications), when my mind lets me leave the house, the fight doesn't end there.

No matter how much I might want my wheelchair to climb the stairs to a residency or festival venue, it just won't.

No matter how much I want outdoor venues or ventilation or some form of Covid safety, no matter how much I wish others would take the ongoing pandemic seriously, they just don't.

No matter how much I want to change the attitudes of people who hear the word 'disabled' and think 'less', I just can't.

There are booksellers and publishers, organisations and individuals, who can't see the relevance of inclusive language and processes, who think they've published one disabled book, so they've done enough.

I'm not saying it's impossible. I'm writing this essay after all (the day before it's due because, #CripTime).

It's just undeniably difficult and frustrating and exhausting and it makes me want to give up. And on those days, I return to what I know. I return to the joys that sustain me.

Voice notes with friends who *get* it. Who've been there too or are in the midst of the mess with me.

The times when my body and mind align, and I can write. The words might pour out or they might be an effort, a trickle. Either way, they're *mine.*

The things I can control: the words on the page. Or, when light sensitivity has kicked in, the sounds of my favourite writing podcasts or audiobooks.

Remembering every acceptance that got me here, every #OwnVoices book I've read, and their authors, who made it through every ableist microaggression and assumption.

On those days, I hold onto the possibility of a world that changes to accommodate us, in all our disabled glory.

Picture this:

The Miles Franklin Award ceremony. So many of the finest writers of so-called Australia gathered in one place.

There's a ramp leading up to the stage, not a stair in sight. The room is well-ventilated and there're Auslan interpreters next to the speakers, in full view. It's a fragrance-free event. There's a quiet space for those who need it. Videos are captioned, service animals are welcomed. People can lie down if they need to, can stim to their heart's content.

Disabled people and our allies, united by our love of creativity, by our understanding of what words can do. All of us safe. All of us welcome.

I believe that's possible, because I've seen how the world can change. How disabled people have fought for our rights – and won. I am only able to write these words – you're only reading them – because of those crip victories.

I am indebted to every disabled writer who has come before me and dared to demand more than they were given, who dared to challenge the status quo.

Because of them, we have children's authors like Kate Foster and Olivia Muscat. We have memoirists like Fiona Murphy and Gayle Kennedy. We have poets like Andy Jackson and Alex Creece, and writers, content creators and advocates like Carly Findlay and Emily Unity.

I hold those disabled truths in my heart, and I write.

Every minute I devote to my craft is a minute of joy and resistance. Even – especially – if it takes me ten times as long as a non-disabled person. Every word I write is another layer of our history, a relic that some future disabled person might read and learn from too.

And, I hope, it's one word closer to our accessible disabled literary utopia.

Joey Harper

Why I'm no longer justifying my special interests: On *Bluey*, cringe culture and systemic ableism

Special interests, for neurodivergent people, are an intense focus or hyperfixation on a particular topic or multiple topics. They can range from popular culture to a certain animal to a particular historical event, but this list is not exhaustive. It becomes a special interest when the individual pursues more information on the topic, whether that be by reading about it, consuming media, or thinking/talking about it with peers. This differs from the neurotypical (those who do not experience autism, ADHD, or other forms of neurodivergence) experience, as autistic special interests help the individual to regulate, create a sense of structure and order in the uncertainty of daily life, offer self-assurance in social situations, and act as a fundamental outlet for overall well-being and happiness.

A lot of my special interests (even before I got a formal diagnosis for autism) were met with confusion and mockery. This is something I never fully understood, especially at a young age. Now, in my infinite wisdom (and after finally getting a diagnosis), I have concluded that this is since a lot of my special interests have revolved around content targeted towards younger audiences. In the past, I was belittled for expressing interest in these things; they were seen as 'too childish'. I was constantly asked, 'How old are you again?' This shamed me into keeping quiet about my interests and caused me to mask my autistic traits more and more. My adolescent adventures on the internet demonstrated to me that I'm not an outlier in this experience.

Growing up on the internet in the 2000s and 2010s was nothing short of horrific, especially if you were in any way 'different'. When

I was around thirteen to fourteen years of age, I began expressing an interest in *My Little Pony*. I thrived on my introduction to fandom culture with a DeviantArt account dedicated to Microsoft Paint drawings of my favourite characters, and by scrolling through YouTube for fan-made music. I didn't feel shame initially; I didn't see anything wrong with being invested in a show maybe aimed at a younger audience, so I had no qualms being open about my art and listening to the aforementioned music in my Year 7 maths classroom. I was subject to ridicule and bullying from my peers, even getting some comments from my teacher. From then on, I started hiding my special interests. I was filled with such a great sense of shame, something that I could not fully comprehend at the time, being undiagnosed.

This was, of course, around the time that mass media attention around a subsection of the fandom, 'Bronies', arose. They usually consisted of older men enjoying and engaging with the show, and in the deeper and darker corners of the internet, sexualising it. Because there existed the problematic and predatory sexualisation of underaged characters in a minority portion of a fandom, broader society seemed to assume that every member of a fandom who did not fit the target age bracket also partook in this unsavoury behaviour. People like me, part of the fandom out of pure enjoyment, were grouped with those who had more sinister intentions, and villainised as a result. With this, a new term entered my vocabulary: cringe.

Cringe culture manifested within online circles as severe judgement and bullying of people partaking in interests that may be out of 'the norm'. I have seen enough 'Epic Feminist Cringe Compilations' to last a lifetime (or two), mostly making a mockery of queer and neurodivergent women. Surprise, surprise: this also had a negative impact on my values and interests. As someone coming to terms with existing in a world skewed out of my favour, seeing other people like me standing up for their rights be referred to as 'cringe' warped my sense of justice. Have interests, but don't be *too* into them, lest you be labelled cringey.

In recent years, interests formally labelled as being 'cringe' are making a resurgence within popular culture. People who were once met with ridicule in the name of cringe are being defended in comment sections of forums with the phrase 'cringe culture is dead'. It suggests a shift away from shaming individuals based on their expressions, hobbies or extracurricular activity, even if they are seen as unconventional or against the norm. This has made both online and offline spaces more welcoming and safer for neurodivergent people who were previously seen as unconventional for their special interests.

However, this cringe counter-culture has changed; what was once a way for neurodivergent people to feel safe engaging in their special interests has been grossly appropriated by neurotypical individuals wishing to justify their problematic interests. For example, people using 'cringe culture is dead' as a justification for problematic fan art (usually involving the sexualisation of a minor). In a similar vein, cringe culture arose from neurotypical people invading safe spaces with a predominant neurodivergent presence and dictating what is socially acceptable. These spaces, which have been a way for autistic people to safely connect over a shared special interest, have been taken over and appropriated by neurotypical people with the intention of bullying and ostracising neurodivergent people.

There seems to be a common pattern wherein neurotypical individuals will not generally be made fun of or bullied for exhibiting certain interests, yet neurodivergent people are often made the butt of the joke. For example, perceptions of adult fans of *My Little Pony* are deeply rooted in infantilisation and sexualisation where this may not necessarily be the case. It is not due to the interests themselves but because the people who show interest in them do it in a way that neurotypical people find uncomfortable or 'cringey'. Hence, the perpetuation of cringe culture being built on the foundations of what I like to call 'acceptable ableism': it's not ableist if the neurodivergent person is being *too* weird, outward or unconventional about their interest. God help you if you are in any way queer as well as neurodivergent.

For the first time in what feels like my whole life, I am surrounded by people who celebrate my interests, even indulge me in them. Being in online spaces where people celebrate my interests, such as interest-specific forums and spaces dedicated to those who are neurodivergent, has been a significant factor in this. As well as this, my friendship and support circles offline are either accommodating of my neurodivergence or are neurodivergent themselves. I owe this in part to *Bluey*, the fun Australian cartoon about dogs, because who doesn't love cartoon dogs? It's no surprise that this show has attracted a large audience of neurodivergent individuals. In fact, one episode depicts ADHD in a respectful and educational manner; who knew this sort of subject matter could be represented in a cartoon for kids? In a way, *Bluey* has helped me relive and reconceptualise my childhood. I see a lot of myself in Bluey's younger sister, Bingo, as a kid with undiagnosed autism (this has not been confirmed by the showrunners but is a common reading of the character). Yet, instead of being met with ridicule and confusion, Bingo and her parents learn to navigate these difficulties together.

By writing about my experiences, I hope that I can work towards dismantling my internalised ableism further, redefine cringe culture and be proud of my special interests. I know who means the most to me if they listen to one of my many info-dumps about Remi Wolf, or rants about *The Owl House* and *Persona* series, or buy me *Bluey* plushies because they thought of me. It's these people who make me feel safe in a world that is often unsafe for neurodivergent people, and it's thanks to them that I have learnt to embrace my special interests.

Acknowledgements

Firstly, we would like to express our gratitude to Michelle Cahill and *Mascara Literary Review* for their championing efforts, recommending writers, and advocating for the emergence of this exciting anthology you now hold. We should also like to give a shout-out to the work of *Mascara Literary Review* as a journal that has highlighted and continues to highlight and support a plethora of distinct and powerful voices from First Nations, refugee and CALD backgrounds. We would also like to thank Dimitra Harvey for assisting and supporting editors and contributors, and to Harriet McInerney and NewSouth Publishing for their warm enthusiasm and generosity of understanding, and for helping this anthology come into the world. We are also grateful for the funding we have received from Creative Australia and all those individuals who have supported in one way or another the birth of this anthology – huge thanks to you. We should also like to thank all of the disabled intersectional writers who submitted their work – it takes a lot of gumption to write your truths and submit them to the process, and it was a privilege reading all of your distinct stories.

Contributors

Mona Zahra Attamimi

Mona is Yemeni-Indonesian, a writer with disability, and lives on the unceded land of the Bediagal people. She lived as a child in Jakarta, Washington DC and Manila, before moving to Australia at age nine. Her poems have been published in various journals and anthologised in the *Contemporary Asian Australian Poets* anthology and *To Gather Your Leaving: Asian diaspora poetry from America, Australia, UK and Europe.* She is the co-founder of the online poetry platform Sun Talks. In 2019, she was the recipient of the Asialink Arts Emerging Writing Residency, in Bandung, Indonesia.

Pat Gia Han Bui

Pat Gia Han Bui is a Vietnamese writer based in Naarm (Melbourne). Growing up in Hanoi, Vietnam, then later Naarm, she explores her multicultural upbringing and female identity, as well as themes of mental health, neurodivergence and trauma. Currently, she is excited by experimenting with ways in which language can be decolonised and decentred from Western traditions of writing, pushing her poetry, fiction and memoir to its breaking point. This is her first professional publication, and when she is not stressing over university deadlines or public transport, she enjoys 4 grams of matcha right before bed and writing in the dead of night.

Hem Sid Chandran (aka Sid)

Sidharth is an Autistic man who spent his early years without a formal means of communication. He attended Autistic schools and completed his schooling at special schools. He has a great curiosity about the nature of Autism and the way it affects him, and wants to make a contribution to the understanding of Autism. In 2023 he published a book, *An Unspoken Story*, documenting his struggles with the severe communication and sensory challenges of Autism. It also deals with his discovery of an alternative system of communication that worked for him. Sidharth grew up in Sydney, where he has spent all of his life. He loves the outdoors and music, as well sports such as skating, swimming and biking. He enjoys writing and considers it to be his vocation. Sidharth has a website at <www.unspokenstory.com.au>.

Sandra Collins

Sandra is a Wiradjuri woman and multimedia community artist who utilises story and improvisation to support her creative works. The focus of her work is to offer opportunities for connection, belonging and strengthening community.

Angela Costi

Angela Costi lives with a rare genetic condition: multiple schwannomatosis. She is the author of six poetry collections. The most recent is *The Heart of the Advocate* (Liquid Amber Press, 2025). Her chapbook *Adversarial Practice*, published by Cordite Poetry Review, was commended in the Wesley Michel Wright Prize 2024. Her poem 'If my writing were a cure' won the University of Canberra's Health Poetry Prize. She lives on unceded Wurundjeri land, and is known as Αγγελική Κωστή among the Cypriot diaspora, her ancestry.

Sharleigh Crittenden

Sharleigh Crittenden is a Wiradjuri writer living and writing on Wangal Country. Her poetry, short fiction and essays have been published in Australian and international publications such as *Island*, *The Suburban Review*, *Portside Review*, *Thread Lit Mag* and *The Rumpus* (among others). Her writing has been recognised in shortlists and prizes, including the inaugural First Nations Storytelling Prize (2023), the Short But Deadly Flash Prize (2024) and the Nakata Brophy Poetry Prize (2024). She is currently writing her debut novel, supported by a 2023 Magabala Creative Grant. In 2024, she was the recipient of a Varuna First Nations Fellowship.

Skye Cusack

Skye Cusack is a Dulgubarra-Yidinji writer, journalist and accidental comedian living in Rubibi (Broome). Skye shares stories that make you laugh, cry, and call your therapist. Common themes in her writing include mental health, disability, fatphobia, existential Blak crises, and people generally making fools of themselves. Her most recent work, a queer rom-com titled *Checked Out*, received a 2025 Elevate Grant, 2025 Varuna First Nations Fellowship and was shortlisted for the 2025 Penguin Write It Fellowship. Her New Adult novel *The Dangers of Just One Person* will be published by Magabala Books in 2027.

Julie Dickson

Julie Dickson (she/her) is a writer and disability advocate based in Naarm. As a person of short stature, she is passionate about increasing positive representation of short stature in literature and the media. She has been awarded Wheeler Centre Hot Desk, Varuna Writer's Space, and Writers Victoria Storming the City fellowships. In 2024, she was the recipient of the Lesley Hall Arts and Disability scholarship. You can find her on Instagram @juliedicksonwrites.

Carly Findlay

Carly Findlay OAM is an award-winning writer, speaker and appearance activist. She received an Order of Australia in 2020 for her work in the literary and disability sectors. She has a master's of communication and a bachelor of ecommerce degree and lives in Melbourne, Australia. Her first book, the memoir *Say Hello*, was released in January 2019. Carly edited the anthology *Growing Up Disabled* in Australia with Black Inc. Books in 2021. She writes on disability and appearance diversity issues for news outlets including

CNN, *Vogue*, ABC, *The Age* and *Sydney Morning Herald* and SBS, as well as contributing to various writing anthologies.

Irina Frolova

Irina Frolova is a first-generation migrant and a neurodivergent writer. She lives on Awabakal Country with her children and fur babies. Irina is studying psychology at Deakin University. Her work explores life and belonging through cultural, feminist, and psychological lenses. Her creative highlights include her first poetry collection *Far and Wild* (Flying Islands, 2021), the second prize in the 2021 Deborah Cass Prize for Writing, and poems recognised in the 2023 University of Canberra VC International Poetry Prize, the 2023 Heroines Women's Writing Prize, and the 2024 Liquid Amber Poetry Prize: Poetry of Change.

Hannah Hall

Hannah Hall is a writer and advocate with a lived experience of disability and complex mental health. She lives and works on the lands of the Wurundjeri Woi Wurrung and the Bunurong peoples of the Kulin Nation. Hannah's work has been published in *The Saturday Paper*, *Archer Magazine* and ABC Everyday. She is co-founder and co-executive director of a not-for-profit arts organisation supporting increased representation for d/Deaf and disabled artists in Australia.

Sam Hamad

Sam Hamad is a Palestinian Australian writer, aspiring geologist, activist, and artist. When he's not looking at rocks at uni, rallying for a free Palestine, or painting his friends, he spends his time writing about anything you can think of – from zombies, snake doctors, and seagull detectives, to stories based on his lived experiences. He has lived with mild Tourette Syndrome for five years, and every day he twitches, shrugs, shakes, squeaks, grunts, and grimaces.

Katie Hansord

Katie Hansord (she/they) is a neurodivergent and queer writer and researcher in Naarm. Her interests include poetry, gender, disability, and print cultures, and her writing has been published in *Mascara, Unusual Work*, *LOR Journal*, and the Long Paddock, *Southerly Journal*.

Joey Harper

Joey Harper (they/them) is a queer, autistic paralegal and aspiring writer living on unceded nipaluna land. They like to experiment with literary form and write both fiction and non-fiction. You can find their musings on Substack.

Jenny Hedley

Jenny Hedley is a neurodivergent writer, Writeability mentor and PhD candidate whose work can be read in many literary journals and in the anthology *Admissions: Voices within Mental Health*. She lives on unceded Boon Wurrung land with her son, and her website can be found at <jennyhedley.github.io/>.

Judith Huang

Judith Huang is a Singaporean–Australian author, poet, science fiction translator, serial-arts-collective-founder and multimedia artist living with a disability. Her first novel, *Sofia and the Utopia Machine*, a speculative fiction novel about immersive worlds, was shortlisted for the Epigram Books Fiction Prize 2017 and Singapore Book Awards 2019. Judith has appeared at the Singapore Writers Festival, George Town Literary Festival, and Perth Poetry Festival. She was a recipient of the WA Poets micro-residency (2024) and the Centre for Stories All Write Fellowship (2024), and has published in *Prairie Schooner, Asia Literary Review*, *Cha*, *QLRS*, *Portside Review* and *Mascara Literary Review*. She was a co-editor of *Perks of Being Dumped*, an anthology of heartbreak writing. She was also shortlisted for the

Pearl Prize 2025. She was commissioned to make the VR artwork *Marcus and the Shadow* for the Perth Institute of Contemporary Arts (PICA) in 2022. Judith founded YAWP!, the longest-running performance poetry competition in Singapore, in 2004, was a co-founder of Spittoon Collective in China, now in over fourteen cities, and is the co-founder of Chilli Jam Open Mic in Perth. She holds a bachelor of arts degree from Harvard University.

Franklyn Hudson

Franklyn Hudson is a queer neurodivergent writer living on unceded lands in Naarm (Melbourne). They have a bachelor of arts degree in creative writing and an honours degree in media and communication from RMIT. They were one of the recipients of the 2021 Ultimo Prize for Poetry and had their poem published in the anthology *Everything, All At Once*. They have also been published in *Meanjin* in the spring 2022 edition. When not writing they can be found obeying the whims of their two very demanding cats.

Priya Gore Johnson

Priya Gore Johnson is an Indian–Australian poet, writer, and aspiring academic based in lutruwita/Tasmania. She is currently completing her honours thesis in English literature at the University of Tasmania with a focus on grief, collaborative survival, and fungal bodies in contemporary speculative fiction. You can find more of her pieces published in the *Mascara Literary Review* and the University of Tasmania's student magazine, *Togatus*.

Mario Licón Cabrera

Mario Licón Cabrera was a Mexican poet and translator based in Sydney since 1992. He published four collections of poetry and translated many Australian poets into Spanish and many Hispanic American poets into English. His most recent publication was *In the small hours / A Atlas horas de la madrugada*, an anthology of poems by Peter Boyle, co-translated with Corina Oproae and Jordi Doce (Nautilus Ediciones, 2025). Mario was affected by advanced muscular dystrophy and retinitis pigmentosa.

CB Mako

CB (cubbie) Mako (they/them) is both a violist and a writer. Based in Naarm, cubbie is one of the violists of the newly formed Inner West Symphony Orchestra. As a writer, cubbie has contributed to the anthologies *Raging Grace: Australian writers speak out on disability*, *Growing Up Disabled in Australia*, *Collisions: Fictions of the future* and *Mascara Literary Review*'s *Resilience*. They have won the Grace Marion Wilson Emerging Writers Competition and have been shortlisted in *Overland*'s Fair Australia Prize and the Lord Mayor's Creative Writing Awards, as well as longlisted in the LIMINAL Fiction Prize. Writing by cubbie appears in *The Suburban Review*, *Peril Magazine* and *Kill Your Darlings*, among other publications.

J Marahuyo

J Marahuyo is a neurodivergent Filipino–Australian award-winning poet residing on Dharug Country. Her debut poetry collection, *crying gorgeously; 4:37am* (WestWords Books, 2025), explores themes of identity, mental health and the power of vulnerability. She was shortlisted for the Newcastle Poetry Prize 2024, won the Writing NSW Varuna Fellowship 2024 and won the Living Stories Prize 2024. Her work can be found in *Cordite Poetry Review*, *The Suburban Review* and *FemAsia*. When she's not writing you can find her pspsp-ing random cats or getting on the wrong train. She can be found on Instagram @j_marahuyo and her website, <www.jmarahuyo.com>.

Carly-Jay Metcalfe

Carly-Jay Metcalfe is a Queensland-based writer of memoir, fiction and creative non-fiction. Her writing has been published in the *Sydney*

Morning Herald, *The Age*, *Australian Women's Weekly*, *Guardian*, *Kill Your Darlings*, and *TEXT Journal*. Carly-Jay's critically acclaimed memoir *Breath* (UQP Books, 2024) won the People's Choice Queensland Literary Award for Queensland Book of the Year. Carly-Jay is a passionate advocate for organ donation and more honest conversations surrounding dying and death.

Akii Ngo

Akii Ngo (they/them) is an international multi-award-winning and multidisciplinary professional, consultant, trainer, educator, and diversity, equity, inclusion and belonging practitioner who is deeply passionate about human rights, disability, accessibility, intersectionality, non-tokenistic representation and all aspects of inclusion and co-design. They have dedicated their life and career to making a positive, sustainable difference to marginalised communities, especially those they are part of. Akii is a proudly multiply disabled, multiply neurodivergent (Autistic, ADHD and C-PTSD), Queer/LGBTIQA+ trans and gender-diverse person of colour from a non-English-speaking refugee background. Akii lives with very complex chronic illnesses and debilitating chronic pain, and has several degenerative physical disabilities. Akii is also a fierce survivor-advocate and activist for violence prevention – one of their main disabilities (spinal injury) is a direct result of intimate partner violence. Akii contributes extensively to community and change-making, offering their lived experience expertise through consulting, advising and presenting, as well as working within the media, fashion and beauty industries as an internationally published model, writer and creative, fighting for improved diverse intersectional representation. Akii can be found on social media @akii_ngo and their website: <www.akiingo.com>.

Ann Nguyen

Born in Kon Tum and raised in Hà Nội, Ann found poetry within the vast tapestry of Vietnamese literature and history. Their family uprooted to move to Naarm (Melbourne) a decade ago, where their lives were forever changed by new language, faces and suffering. Ann writes with their ancestors behind them, meditating on racial grief, joy and interbeing.

Arty Owens

Arty Owens (they/them) is a queer, neurodivergent and chronically ill writer based in Naarm (Melbourne). A psychiatrist once told Arty, 'You've lived quite the impressive life, although most of my clients are six-year-olds.' Their craft is informed by their illness, anxiety and devastating awkwardness. Through their non-fiction work they invite you to experience the way they navigate the world as a disabled creative. Their accolades include the Varuna Residential Fellowship, the Wheeler Centre Hot Desk Fellowship, Creative Australia grant recipient and a finalist in the 2023 Wyndham Art Prize.

Ethan Patrick

Ethan Patrick is a writer, freelance editor and creative writing tutor who lives and works on the unceded lands of the Wurundjeri people of the Kulin Nation, with an extremely friendly labrador and not-so-friendly cat. He's also meandering his way through a creative writing PhD at the University of Melbourne, with his research focusing on the representation of physical disability in fantasy novels and their influence on societal attitudes towards disability. As part of his thesis, he's writing a fantasy novel featuring a disabled protagonist. Ethan has published a few pieces concerning his lived experience of disability, the most recent of which, 'Disability Representations', was published by the University of Sheffield's iHuman blog.

Laura Pettenuzzo

Laura Pettenuzzo is a disabled bibliophile, writer and speaker living on Wurundjeri Country. She has a Master of Professional Psychology from Monash University and runs an accessible communications business called All for Access. Her writing explores the impacts of ableism and mental illness, and celebrates the power of self-acceptance and disability pride. Her words have appeared in places such as *Archer Magazine*, *Griffith Review*, ABC Lifestyle, SBS and *The Age*. You can usually find her with a cup of tea in her hands and her cat, Giles, on her lap.

Rosie Putland

Rosie Putland (she/her) is a proudly disabled, queer person living in regional lutruwita/Tasmania. She is a storyteller and consultant working to make the digital world a more accessible place. You will find her most happy knitting and surrounded by ducks.

Ariel Riveros

Ariel Riveros, born in Santiago, Chile, is a writer living on Gadigal land. Ariel won the 2016 Schizophrenia Fellowship of NSW Poetry Prize. His first chapbook, *Commoning* (2018), was published by Vagabond Press, Sydney. His literary work appears in various publications and anthologies. Ariel is currently an NDIS participant with interests in salsa dance, swimming and classical guitar.

Paris Rosemont

Paris Rosemont is an Asian-Australian, LGBTQIA+, neurodivergent poet and author of *Banana Girl* (2023) and *Barefoot Poetess* (2025). Her edgy, distinctive poetry has been widely published and awarded. *Banana Girl* was shortlisted by the Association for the Study of Australian Literature for the 2024 Mary Gilmore Award. It was also shortlisted for Poetry Book Awards 2024 in Australia, Greece,

USA and UK, and was awarded 'Distinguished Favorite' in the NYC Independent Press Award 2025 (USA). Paris's niche is in performance poetry. She has graced stages at events and festivals in almost every state/territory within Australia and has also performed internationally. Paris was selected to be a judge for the Western Australian Premier's Book Awards 2025, and is currently appointed as a member of the Randwick City Council Arts and Culture Advisory Committee. Paris may be found on Instagram @msparisrose.

Marina Sano

Marina Sano (she/her) is a Japanese and Australian critic, publishing freelancer, and bookseller. She co-founded Amplify Bookstore and is an advocate for more diverse and representative publishing. She holds a bachelor's degree in English literature and a master's in publishing and communications, and has been published in *Kill Your Darlings*, the *Australian Multilingual Writing Project* and *Books+Publishing*. She lives and works on unceded Wurundjeri land.

Kerri Shying

Kerri Shying is a poet of Wiradjuri and Chinese family, publishing across many journals and anthologies. They are the author of a bilingual pocketbook of poems, *sing out when you want me* (2017), *Elevensies* (2018) and *Knitting Mangrove Roots* (2019), as well as their current collection *Know Your Country* (2021), through Puncher & Wattmann. They are one of the editors of the anthology *Raging Grace: Australian writers speak out on disability*, published by Puncher & Wattmann, 2024, and one of five Australian poets featured in the international anthology *Versus Versus: 100 Poems by deaf, diabled and neurodivergent poets*, Bloodaxe Books, 2025. Kerri has been convener and mentor at Write Up/WU, a free arts/writing group for people living with disability, for eight years. They live with disability in Newcastle, NSW, with their famous dog Max Spangly.

Ari Spanos

Ari Spanos (they/them) is a young creative living on unceded Bidjigal land. They are neurodivergent (Autistic, ADHD, bipolar) queer and genderqueer, and come from a Greek family. They work in allied health from a neuro-affirming, LGBTQIA+ informed and fat-positive approach, as well as developing LGBTQIA+ inclusive practice training. They are new to formal writing, but have always been drawn to stories, poetry and songs to help them express and understand their own and others' experiences.

TextaQueen

Wielding tools other than their namesake felt-tip, TextaQueen presents creative non-fiction, satire, and poetry about othered bodies, trauma, land and their relationships. Their writing has appeared in *Cordite*, *Meanjin*, *Peril*, Disability Arts Online, and on tour with Sister Spit (USA). Texta received a 2023 Writers Victoria Writeability Fellowship for mentorship with Narungga poet Natalie Harkin.

BS Windon

BS Windon is a neurodivergent author of Wiradjuri heritage based in Naarm (Melbourne). Unable to settle on just one genre of writing, he wields them all with reckless abandon. His creative non-fiction led to him being a finalist for the Writers Prize in the 2024 Melbourne Prize for Literature, and he is a previous winner of *Griffith Review*'s Emerging Voices competition. Beau is doing his PhD in the 'Aesthetic Form of Neurodivergent Literary Memoir' – which is WILD because he flunked his high school English classes. If Beau could be any animal, he would be a chocolate egg – the kind with a toy hidden inside. Find him (if you dare) at <www.beauwindon.com>.

Misbah Wolf

Misbah Wolf (she/they) is a CALD neurodivergent multidimensional artist living in Naarm (Melbourne). She writes books and poetry, performs, teaches, researches, and creates. Her creative work, which explores love, be/longing, ghosts, wildness (anything Gothic), has appeared in many places – just Google. Misbah is actually Mirabel Contrary (very unmasked actually) and performs in her Gothic cabaret band The Shimmering Dark, blending music and surreal theatre.

www.ingramcontent.com/pod-product-compliance
Lightning Source LLC
LaVergne TN
LVHW100922110826
845155LV00036B/49
* 9 7 8 1 7 6 1 1 7 0 4 7 8 *